Confessions of a Graphic Designer

Surviving and thriving in the graphic design, illustration and advertising world 1975-2017

©2017 – John Franklin Green

Memoirs and a guide for those who are in the business, about to enter the business *and those even thinking about* entering the business.

This book also contains practical tips and advice from a professional creative director, art director, designer, illustrator and business owner for over forty years.

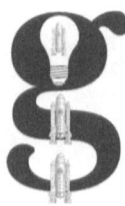

This book dedicated to the memory
of the late Donald J. Moore Sr.
my first employer at D.J. Moore Advertising in NY
and from whom I learned so much.
He was a great professional,
a true gentleman and my mentor.

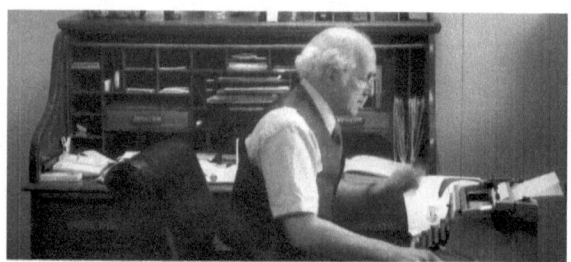

c. 1972 in his office.

See other books by this author at:
www.jgreenbooks.com

PLEASE NOTE:
All of the examples in this book reproduced
in black and white because of the budget constrictions of
"print on demand" paperback books.

*If you want to see color, renditions
and much more please visit:*
www.creativecolleagues.com

CONTENTS

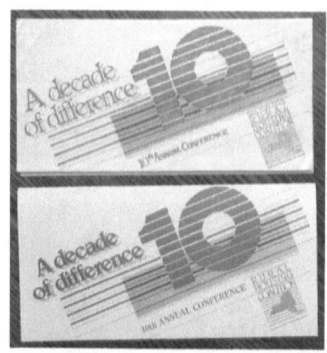

IN THE BEGINNING...

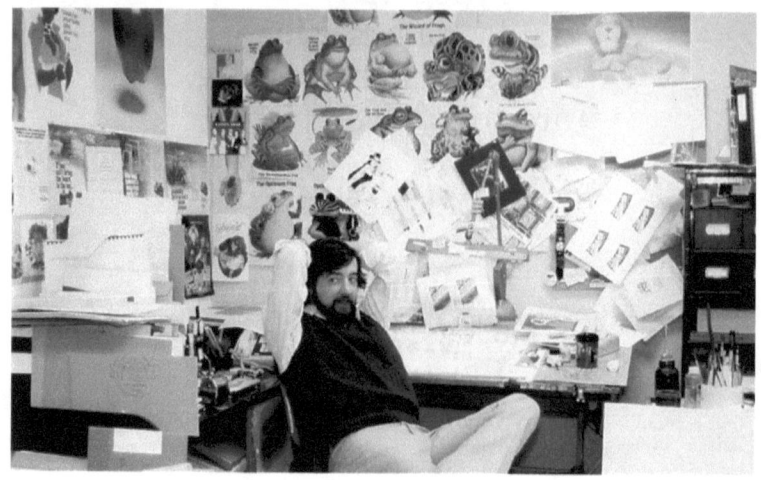

...there were drawing boards, x-acto knives, rubber cement, markers, pencils, ruling pens, illustration board, amberlith and coffee - lots of coffee. Only the coffee remains.

The above left is the only a marker rendered layout for client approval, remaining that I have, along with the finished printed brochure. The tools of the profession have changed but the concepts, ideas and creative process are the same...

INTRODUCTION

He walked out on stage before about one hundred and twenty eighteen-year old freshman art students, clasped his hands behind his back and started pacing back and forth looking us over while occasionally stroking his goatee. His jet-black mustache, goatee, and hair combed back and slick combined with his sharp aquiline nose made him appear to be a caricature of Satan in a sport jacket, white shirt and tie. Professor Jack Slutzky, ex New York City art director stopped, faced us and said - "So, you all want to be prostitutes?"

Some of the guys chuckled under their breath, rolled their eyes or sat silently staring. Some of the girls blushed or squirmed in their seats. Whatever the reaction, like a good headline or graphic, he got our attention. The year was 1971 and I was in his class entitled Creative Sources. He went on to explain to we aspiring graphic designers (it was also still referred to back then in many quarters as commercial art), art directors and illustrators that what we were about to try to enter into a career had nothing to do with "art." We would ultimately wind up creating and directing visual art paid for, *and most often controlled by other people for money.* What we personally liked or thought of as our skilled creative domain meant little. *Doing others, bidding for money was the definition of a prostitute.* Long before I finished a forty-year career as an art director, creative director, copywriter, graphic designer, illustrator, web designer and studio owner, *I learned that that he was right.*

Toward the end of my career, I had an argument with a female relative of mine who adamantly exclaimed that I should not refer to myself as that. It was demeaning and not accurate she said. I was informed that if I wanted to, I should refer to myself if not by any of my official titles, a mercenary. It would be a better choice of words than 'prostitute.' Although she never really understood it, or chose not to, I explained the difference with this analogy:

An organized crime boss wants someone dead. A *mercenary* "hit man" is told: "I want 'John Doe' killed by the end of this month and I don't care how you do it as long as it can't be traced back to me." A fee is agreed upon and when the mission is accomplished, the fee is paid.

The alternate scenario runs as follows: "I want 'John Doe' killed by a safe dropping on him from a fourth floor window on Main Street in Sandusky, Ohio while wearing a red cardigan sweater, walking his dog and smoking a cigar at 11:15 a.m. on the thirteenth of the month." The fact that the subject of the assassination lived in Chicago, doesn't own a dog and never smokes *anything* is irrelevant. To earn the fee all conditions must be met. This is more like prostitution.

Alternatively, to put it in the oldest profession's terms: "we will have sex the way I want it and only the way I want it." *This is called prostitution.*

Now the "commercial artists" of the world, much like prostitutes, can get along well, make money and have long if sometimes frustrating careers as long as they can grasp this basic nature of their profession. Moreover, we rarely are arrested. Along with this comes the basic acceptance that the client, the client's spouse, every employee of their company and the client's nephew who took and art class during one semester in junior college out rank you. Learn to live with it if you value your sanity and bank account.

Within these pages, I will explain to you how to not only cope with this reality without eating your own young or becoming hopelessly insane, *but also how to develop concepts and mindsets to survive and thrive* in no matter what field of creative art endeavor you are pursuing, want to pursue or are just beginning to.

Before I do that I want to pass along a valuable lesson on the term "creativity" I learned in the previously mentioned class called Creative Sources at Rochester Institute of Technology. One of the class assignments given was to create a planet that was unique, drawing on nothing we knew about or existed. The assignment was to be completed, in written and visual format. We all worked diligently and furiously for a week and turned in our wonderfully creative brilliance. We all received an F as a grade. Jack was gracious and later canceled the bad grade because the assignment was basically impossible, which was exactly his point. All creativity is about is rearranging things that already exist to achieve a specific task, much like a chef combining food elements in a different way to achieve a hopefully good tasting dish. We can *create* nothing. The chef does not create the various elements he uses, proteins, spices, oils, starches, fruits and vegetables he merely recombines them in a different way and in different proportions. *This is what he wanted us to understand.*

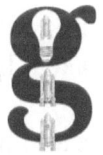

A FURTHER NOTE ON THE "CREATIVE PROCESS"

The old maxim that "creativity is one percent *inspiration* and ninety-nine percent *perspiration."* is true. No matter what the project, we must do our homework and research, make lists, doodle, sketch, take notes and think hard often in multiple directions. When time permits, we need to take a break, long or short to let this work digest and percolate. This many times is when the "inspiration" happens. Sometimes it doesn't and we have to go back and sweat some more and soldier on.

From personal experience, I can tell you with great certainty that great ideas do NOT come from doodles on cocktail napkins or the swirling bottom of a bong or a bowl. Earnest Hemingway famously opined that you should "write drunk and edit sober." The trouble is that when sober and editing you often find that the artificial inspiration and ideas are mostly crap. The same is true in the visual arts and it can also eventually lead you sometimes into a personal abyss from which you may be lucky to survive and recover.

Many inspirations and insights more often come from the bedroom, breakfast table or the bathroom. When we are distracted or relaxed doing the ordinary, mundane activities of life that we all must do all of the perspiration pays off seemingly out of the blue. Then we return to work and make it happen.

Boardrooms, conference rooms and brainstorming sessions can be useful for information gathering but from my experience, they seldom lead to an immediate, tangible solution to the project at hand. Creativity like leadership is usually a singular affair. I once sat in a conference room with the controller, marketing manager, sales manager and several others for hours discussing how to put together a design concept for a brochure about a company that made heavy industrial die cutting machines. My brain eventually went numb and I was very relieved when I got to the parking lot to start the drive back to my office. In the forty minutes, it took to make the drive I had it almost entirely designed and visualized in my head. The conference was not a waste of time because it fed the beast with information, but as a way to work out the structure, concept and design, it was *not* helpful. The percolation time in the car was the really essential part.

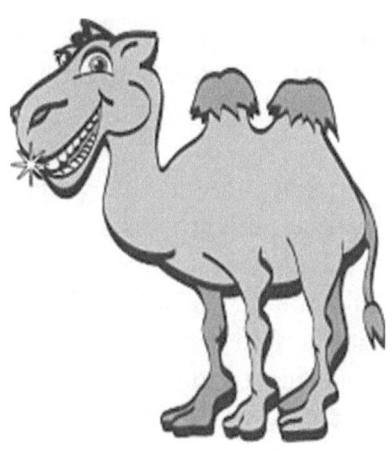

What is the definition of a camel? I often ask this of colleagues and friends. The answer is: "a horse that was designed by a committee." Each member of a committee or review group is asked for an opinion. Not wanting to appear *not* to be doing his or her job, they feel compelled or pressured to put forth a suggestion or an "improvement." Often the "Chinese menu" method is applied to this. "Pick one from column A and one from column B." If you have submitted several design options, this translates into: "We like version B the best, but can you use the headline font from version A, the colors of version C and the illustration from version D?" They rarely understand that any concept is a carefully blended combination of elements that are calculated to work in unison with each other. These same people would never think of wearing their favorite plaid shirt with their best-striped pants and polka dot tie to a business meeting. Hopefully. The resulting camel comes from suggestions like: "Can we make the head bigger?" ... "How about a water storage feature?" ... "It needs bigger hooves." ... "Make the tail smaller with a bushy tassel." ... Well, you get the idea.

When doing opinion polls or mini focus group studies I always just ask; "Which version would you buy?" Never an open-ended question like: "What do you think?" The last question simply invites a torrent of good intentioned suggestions, which are mostly useless and lead to mediocrity.

Later on in my career, I also found that revisiting work done for similar projects helped fuel the process and will save a lot of time. Out takes or rejected ideas often formed the nucleus or at least individual elements for the new project at hand. Most of the time, we will develop several design or creative options for the client to review. Only one is typically decided on but the others need not go to waste – or discarded.

For example - I once devised an ad campaign for Vintage brand seltzer in Pennsylvania to encourage consumers to add Vintage seltzer to juices, powdered drinks or concentrates to "add a splash of sparkle." The campaign was never used for lack of funding. Two decades later, in 2016 while designing labels for Foodtown store brand seltzers they asked for catchy phrases to be added to the label. They loved the phrase, it became the tag line and it helped sell the designs *and* the product.

Computerization aided this technique immensely. I keep well-organized archives of all projects I have done for easily recalled access. Because of this, I have a reputation for speed in addition to good concept and design. Recycling good ideas and graphics works well in today's world of: *"we need it yesterday, if not sooner."*

TECHNOLOGY

I will deal only with concepts in these pages because by time you read this, the technology being used is already obsolete and will be soon replaced and/or improved. When I started in the business almost everything was done by hand or with film. Concepts were presented on paper using pencils, pens, markers and occasionally augmented by chewing gum, scotch tape and spit. Production art for printers and media was painstakingly created using films, paste-ups, mechanical art, photostats, type galley proofs, overlays, photographic prints, transparencies and slides. I have cut acres of amberlith in my time and am pretty sure it doesn't even exist anymore and equally sure that few people reading this have even heard of it. Video and still photography was done on film. About one third of the way into my career, personal computers with design programs and other tools such as Adobe Illustrator and Adobe Photoshop took over. Film was replaced with digital technology not only for images but also for printing and video and presentations. Airbrushes were replaced by photo retouching programs. Custom hand wrought illustrations and expensive studio or location photography were supplemented or supplanted, with stock digital photos and art. The ability and skill to draw still has its advantages. I once had a client ask where I "found" the illustrations I used on some packaging. He was astounded when I told him that I drew them.

No professional colleague I ever met has complained about the new technology, including myself. It has, for the most part, made our job easier, faster and better. If you are young and reading this I have no idea what technology will follow but you will learn it and adapt to it just like artisans of old moved from clay tablets to papyrus. Tools of the time, but just tools nonetheless. The current technology of any given time is and will always be just a tool of that time.

The basic concepts of successful design, advertising and communication however, do not change as long as human beings are the recipients of the message and purpose. I will further constrain this work primarily to various printed media but will touch on some other media such as web sites. Since my experience with animation and broadcast media is limited except as general adverting principles are concerned I will only comment on them regarding general principles of communication. If you have read this far or purchased this book in hope of becoming the recipient of a CLIO award, I apologize and suggest you request a refund. As a side bar to this, research shows that most award winning commercials, designs and other ads most of the time, are dismal failures in the marketplace when it comes to actually selling the product or service.

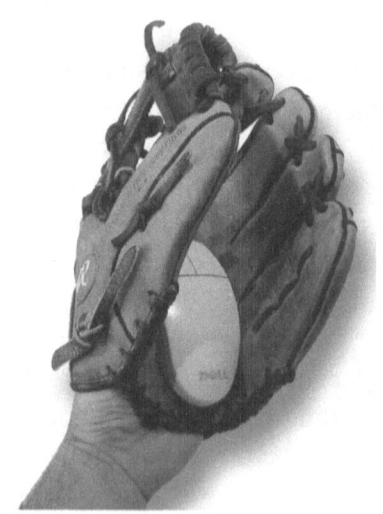

GETTING STARTED

Many students, including myself, start with a passion for a particular art form or career path in mind. In my case, I wanted to be a professional illustrator. Celebrities will tell you at award ceremonies to follow your passion relentlessly until you succeed without ever reminding you that for everyone at the top there are thousands or millions who fail with that approach. Taking advantage of *opportunities* that come along is the best way to keep moving forward even if it is not exactly the direction you had in mind or pigheadedly want to pursue.   Many times those opportunities will eventually lead you where you want to go or more often than not lead you to another interest, which is just as rewarding and satisfying.

In my case, an opportunity presented itself to me only one day out of college to secure a job as an art director for a small advertising agency, which specialized in print oriented business-to-business advertising. I had to decide whether to accept the job or start pounding the pavement, portfolio in hand looking for illustration assignments. I chose to take the job and consequently was only three days unemployed right out of school – and two of those days were Saturday and Sunday! I also accepted a rather low starting salary instead of one that an inflated ego would have rejected. Three months later once I had proved satisfactory to my employer, he jumped my pay dramatically. In the first four months on the job I learned more than in four years in college and in the course of my ten year employment with the agency I did plenty of illustration which I conveniently art directed myself and developed and understanding and the skills to implement good advertising, art direction and graphic design. The net result was:

1. I became a professional illustrator as planned.

2. Found a new interest in advertising.

3. I honed my graphic design skills and also worked for the first time in package design.

After a brief stint of eight months at another agency as the de facto creative director as well as art director, another opportunity arose which led me to start my own business, which I never would have been able to do successfully without the ten plus years advancing my craft.

One day while art directing a photo shoot for a major beverage company for which I had done all of the design work as well as being the account executive another opportunity presented itself. The client contact who was attending the session took me aside and said: "We'll go wherever you go … hint, hint." The decision to start on my own was a no-brainer because I not only did not fit in with the agency but also the annual billings for that client far exceeded my annual salary. This was 1985. That client as well as many others came on board as well as many employees over the course of the next decade. I eventually shed the overhead of employees and a mortgage on an office building and wound up in Arizona where I made well over 100K annually until I slid into semi-retirement in 2011. That original client is incidentally still with me even as I write this.

Now the point of the above is not so much to chronicle my career as to encourage the readers of this book to consider taking advantage of opportunities that may arise randomly and often unplanned whenever it seems prudent do so and sometimes even when it seems downright scary. There has seldom been any path I have experienced or read about that is direct to success and fulfillment. If you know of one, I will be happy to hear about it. This also leads to the next topic:

FINDING YOUR NICHE

Niche marketing is a term for finding a narrow but lucrative market for a product or service that does not to appeal to everyone but has great appeal and sometimes generates great profits from a relatively small sector of the population. Careers most often follow that path as a result of taking advantage of the aforementioned opportunities when they come up or by slowly evolving in a direction.

For example: in my career, illustration that was the original goal never exceeded 30% of my business volume although it was the most enjoyable for me. Even though my company did many forms of advertising (which was my second greatest passion) and graphic design, my concentration through circumstance in the soft drink industry, especially packaging, rapidly became my niche because of the relatively narrow field and my growing expertise in it. Although we did advertising and promotion for the firm, *referrals* became the major source of business growth and revenue. I was and still am, fairly well known within what is a small segment of a large business sector.

What you need to succeed is to find or stumble into your personal niche. This is especially true in today's world of specialization in *almost every* industry or service sector. The days of the "jack of all trades" commercial artist are almost history. Illustrators for generations have been hired mostly for select styles or genres. Agencies and studios hire designers and art directors that *fit their niche* clientele and clients don't want to hire someone who has to learn their business on the fly. That can be an expensive exercise for them *and you.*

There have been countless books, articles and web pages devoted to these subjects so keep in mind that this is, of course, my personal and professional advice on these subjects. Developed over a long career, they have worked well for me. My goal was to make a reasonably good living, which I did and as a result had time to pursue other passions and responsibilities like painting, writing, leather work, coaching youth baseball and raising a family.

The following chapters will deal with my experience in the various areas that I am most experienced in with practical and career business tips along the way:

- Advertising
- Graphic Design
- Package Design
- Illustration
- Collateral
- Websites

ADVERTISING
The second oldest profession.

Before I begin this chapter, I would also highly recommend that you read this book, which might take some finding:

"Ogilvy on Advertising" ©1983 by David Ogilvy
Despite its date it is widely regarded by many professionals including myself as the "Bible" of the advertising industry written by a man who started selling penny postcard direct response advertising in Scotland and went on to build one of the largest and most successful Advertising Agencies in the world. The basic principles he lays down are as valid today as they were over 30 years ago.

Some people seem to think SELL is a dirty four-letter word or something to be ashamed of. "I'm not trying to sell you anything I just want to give you some information about..." At this point, I usually interrupt the person on the phone or standing in my doorway and tell them that if they aren't trying to sell me something they really aren't doing their job and their employer should fire them or at least cut their pay. Or, I ask them if is this is how they have been told or coached to do their job. Often it is. I gently go on to tell them that selling is the second oldest profession. It has been making the world go around since the first cave man, Oog, extolled the excellent quality of his spear and tried to convince the cave man in the next cave over, named Ugg that it was worth two clubs, a saber-tooth tiger pelt and a knife in trade.

Advertising in its myriad forms since the earliest hand drawn sign to television and the internet is the business of selling without the direct cave to cave, door to door or the ubiquitous telephone sales call. When you are assigned to create an advertisement, whether it takes the form of a print media ad, brochure, poster, flier, direct mail piece, website, internet ad or any other communication vehicle - your job is to sell something. Whether it is a product, service, vacation destination or to convince someone that recycling or going green is the best way to help save our planet. Later on, I will expand on the unique benefits and drawbacks of the many forms graphic communication take but in most cases, the same basic principles apply to all. As it applies to concept, copy or graphics, I will refer to it as the 1 - 2 – 3 method of making it work.

There are four basic modes of advertising:

• Consumer advertising:

This is what most people think of when they think of advertising. It is what we are bombarded with daily via television, billboards, magazines, newspapers, internet pop ups, radio, movie theaters etc. A company is aiming at consumers, that is, the general public or a defined segment of it, to purchase a product, service, idea or any combination thereof. It is the type of advertising career most beginners or students generally aspire to. Often however, they find other equally interesting options with more available jobs and opportunities in other modes.

• Business to business advertising:

This is a large and often unknown aspect of advertising. Once known as industrial advertising, it is less glamorous and often financially less appealing but is in some ways a much larger field than consumer advertising. In this mode, businesses aim to convince *other* businesses to buy or use their products or services. This form generally appears in specialty trade publications and collateral materials (brochures, sell sheets, flyers etc.) distributed within the industry they are used for. Several examples are shown in this book. One *(the one with the cute baby)* ran in *Dermatology* magazine and *The Journal of the American Medical Association* to sell health professionals hypoallergenic surgical gloves to practitioners whose skin is sensitive to latex. Another *(the one with the dinosaur)* ran in several electronics manufacturing magazines including *Electronics Test*. The product specifically pre-tested printed circuit boards for common errors so they could be fixed before they went on to more time consuming and expensive functional testing. These ads are not seen by the general public unless someone is involved in a specific business and sees them in specialty magazines, web sites, trade shows and brochures.

Many ad agencies (including the one I started with) and studios specialize in this type and many freelance art directors and designers do this as well because they have experience in that form.

• Public Service advertising:

This is as its name implies, generally aimed at the public to make them aware of a problem, good cause, or a social/environmental concern. It can be a very rewarding career but is way more limited in availability than the previous two. Many consumer or business-to-business agencies and studios will however do this type, often at no charge, if the firm strongly believes in the cause or to gain favorable publicity.

• Political advertising:

This form is generally the lowest breed in the business. *Character assassination, gross distortions and out and out lies are the norm.* In other advertising venues, this would lead to law suits, penalties and total loss of credibility but political organizations seem to escape this under the guise of opinion and the protection of the First Amendment of the United States Constitution.

Every election cycle also sees the curious phenomena of

apparently fungal growths, fertilized by egos and bullshit that sprout on every street corner aimed at name recognition that has been the grand master of electioneering ever since elections were invented.

I have dallied with this form and I can tell you without hesitation that if you do enter this arena, be very sure to get paid in advance for your services. Losers of elections are notorious for not paying their bills! Winners seem also to forget their financial obligations too along with their campaign promises.

Television/Radio

Although I did a small amount of TV ad work early in my career, I spent the vast majority of it in print advertising so I will confine this section to observations and the gleaned knowledge of others on the subject.

The same principles of print apply to TV except you have motion, sound and a very limited amount of time to get your point across. And you have a greater opportunity to waste a lot more money if you fail to do this because video production and air time in astronomically expensive. You are also likely to be a smaller part of the team because of the number of people involved like account executives, brand managers, media buyers, art directors, writers, researchers, directors, camera people, editors, mixers, make up people, stylists, special effects teams and the caterers on the set.

There can be some excitement off camera too. I was once art directing a TV spot for soft drinks in a loft on 32nd street in Manhattan. The catered food was excellent and we were taking a break to enjoy it. As I was talking to my boss at the time and the client we heard what sounded like a gun shot from behind a partition on the set. We all turned in that direction only to see the prop man emerge soaked in root beer and a look of dismay on his face. He had been trimming a camera perfect label on a 2-liter plastic bottle that had been sitting under hot lights for some time and he accidentally scored the bottle with a sharp blade. The pressure of the carbonation exploded the bottle.

Celebrities and entertaining commercials do not do a great job of selling anything. They may win CLIO awards but those award winners are seldom successful in ringing any cash registers. Viewers often remember the clever commercial or the star, but just as often can't recall the product! One historic exception to this was the introduction of Miller Lite beer. A product before its time named Gablinger's diet beer had tried and failed to make headway in the marketplace. Nobody was interested in the term "diet" when it came to drinking beer. Miller presented two retired baseball stars that sat on bar stools arguing back and forth. "Tastes great!" says one ... "Less filling!" countered the other. Miller Lite was a huge success and new product category was born. Light beers by the way; now outsell regular beers to this day.

We often scoff at the "but wait... there's more!" commercials but the truth of the matter is that they SELL a lot of products, some of them poor, but many excellent and useful. "And if you order NOW, we'll also include..." "And all of this for only $19.95!" They work.

Get attention in a meaningful way, communicating clearly and then asking for a response is still the key to success. "Try it, buy it, stop by a store near you, contribute, click on our website, call now, order now, get more information, vote for, be more"... and you have a better than average opportunity to succeed.

The 1-2-3 approach to overall concept:

1. Find out who you are selling to! For example, something that motivates a millennial 23 year old is way different than something that will appeal to the senior citizen audience, a professional, children, or an engineer. Gender is also very important. Despite the ongoing social development of the equality of the sexes, women and men have different preferences and react differently to words and graphics. Ignoring these gender norms can cause failure. If you are trying to sell feminine protection to female motorcycle enthusiasts, showing a woman blazing over rocky terrain on a trail bike with a powerful masculine typeface in the headline while convincing her your product offers all day, all condition, comfort and protection will get her attention better than showing two women sipping cocktails at a bistro.

The overall concept, words *and visual approach* must be tailored to your audience in order to sell them anything or convince them of a worthy cause to support. All elements from the choice of typography, visual to overall attitude are important and must work together.

Often as a designer, much of this has been determined before you are called in on the assignment, BUT be sure to inquire of the client, your boss or the account executive before you pick up a pencil or click a mouse. You would be surprised how often these simple questions have not been clarified. If you or they know the answers, you are off to a good start. If they don't know, ask them to find out because it will not only allow you to do a better job, it will make you seem smarter and more tuned in. And more respected.

2. Find out everything you can about what you are communicating! What is it, what does it do or not do, why is it important, and why should anyone care? Is it bigger, better, faster, cheaper, more desirable, or different than the competition? What are the important features or facts? But of all these things, *the most important* is what I call WFM: What's in it For Me? *Features are fine but benefits are best.* People are motivated by what they perceive is the benefit to them. Will they feel better, save money, be happier, be more attractive or get the job done better or easier?

As in #1 above, a good account executive or copywriter should have the answers to these questions and it should be apparent in the words they wrote. If they don't - ask. If you are working directly with the client, ask them! If nobody knows either refuse to start or better yet do the homework yourself if it is possible. Sometimes, as was often the case in my career, I was both the copywriter and designer, but in either case, your design approach should reflect and emphasize the WFM's.

All of this must be integrated into the whole message package and tailored to the space and reaction time allotted. For example - an eight-page brochure allows for more space than a fractional banner ad on the internet BUT the same principles apply.

3. Find out the expected Response/Reaction - All of the above leads to the conclusion of: What response from the viewer is expected and desired? Should they call, click, e-mail, come to the store, buy it, contribute, conform, protest, clip the coupon, send in the response card, order today? *This is the **call to action** and is the most important part.* Don't forget this and don't treat it as a small afterthought or assume it is obvious. Make it look important because it is! To make an analogy to the dating scene: you can look your best, talk about your best qualities and be sincere and honest, but if you don't ask them out for a date, *nothing is going to happen.*

We are bombarded by advertising, messages, pop ups, billboards, bus cards, bumper stickers, jingles, jangles and bangles more today than ever in history. Getting noticed, getting the message across and getting a response can be difficult but it is our job! Doing some artsy, trendy poorly conceived or ill thought out piece of graphic communication is a gross waste of time, talent and money. This leads us to the next set of 1-2-3's.

MAKING IT COME TOGETHER AND WORK.

Just what is an idea that works? The term "works" or "does this work?" is used endlessly and often without meaning or measure and often by people who are clueless or unable to articulate their definition of what works.

The answer is as simple as 1-2-3. "Work" means a communication solution that accomplishes at least three things:

1. COMMAND ATTENTION

To get someone's attention is almost always the main object of the headline and the *predominant* visual. In both cases you can SHOUT, whisper, SHOCK, amuse, entice, seduce, SCARE, inform, cajole, beg, beautify, charm or beg in any combination but the purpose is always to capture the viewer's attention *in a way that is relevant* to what you are selling. You can't sell anything unless you get someone's attention first. Considering you have about 1.3 seconds to do this, it better be strong and simple.

Some years ago, I collected ads for a trade publication whose main tag line and theme was that they were "The big frog in a small pond" meaning that their publication was the most important and largest in a very small select industry and that is why advertisers should buy ads in their magazine. The series used the visual **shout** approach. The headline was supported by imaginative, distorted and LARGE illustrations of frogs. Body builder flexing frogs, college educated frogs, purple frogs, pink frogs, egghead frogs, frogs doing the most outrageous things *and all related to the supporting headline*. The ads were amusing, consistent and most of all caught the attention of advertising agency media buyers and account executives.

Shock can be effective as long as it pertains to the message. A beached whale on a desert mesa, a tortured dog, or a girl with a cleft palate certainly grab attention but only work if you can relate it to the message like drought conditions worsen in California - please use water wisely, donate to the SPCA, or support children born with this condition for just a very small donation.

A classic ad campaign for Volkswagon in the 1960s by Doyle, Dane Bernbach Advertising is as relative and effective today used the **whisper** technique. A small photo of the car floated in a large area of empty white space. The two-word headline read: "Think small." Visually it used a lot of white space to stand out from the clutter of other ads. It sold a lot of VW Beetles!

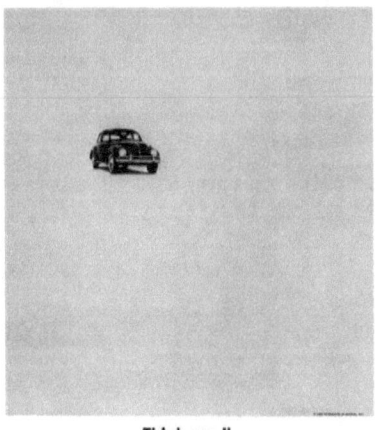

Think small.

In a time when most automobiles were BIG and flashy, this concept caught attention. The body copy extolled the economy of initial price and fuel economy.

A common and mostly over used and misused **entice** attention getter is SEX. Unless you are selling sex related items like birth control, lingerie, Vegas vacations, fragrances or erectile dysfunction treatments or services, using babes in bikinis, big boobs, bodacious booties, ripped abs or sexy male chests may grab and eye or two or ten, BUT that is about it. Ogle the picture but then move on. I have seen this in countless uses over the years. One that stands out in memory for this purpose was an internet banner ad series for a language-learning program. Big boobs and low cut cleavage was supposed to get you to click to get more information and buy the program. These ran for quite a while and while I am not privy to the sales results, I did note that the switched to visuals and headlines that related more to ease of learning and how the program actually worked. To entice the reader, you want to show or say something that is unusual or invites a question.

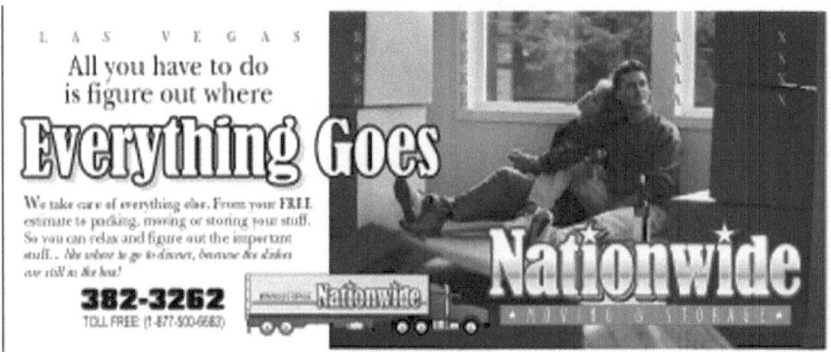

Entice. Everyone has moved at least once and knows the hassles. The couple is attractive and relaxed, the headline has a small amount of double entendre and the truck illustration points directly to the company logo.

Judicious **borrowing** can also work wonders especially on a smaller budget. One of my favorite and effective "borrows" was an award-winning ad I did for a health insurance company. At the time American Express had pounded the airwaves and print media saying "the American Express Card, don't leave home without it." The bold and simple headline I wrote for the ad read: "The OTHER card you shouldn't leave home without." The visual was simply their membership identification card. The body text, written by an agency copywriter, explained how extensive their network coverage was so that you were covered in many places when traveling and if you happened to get sick or injured.

Another was a series of ads and airport posters for a hotel chain that featured photos of guests enjoying the many amenities. The bold headline read: "Check out any time you like but you won't want to leave." It was a permissible play on the popular Eagles song "Hotel California."

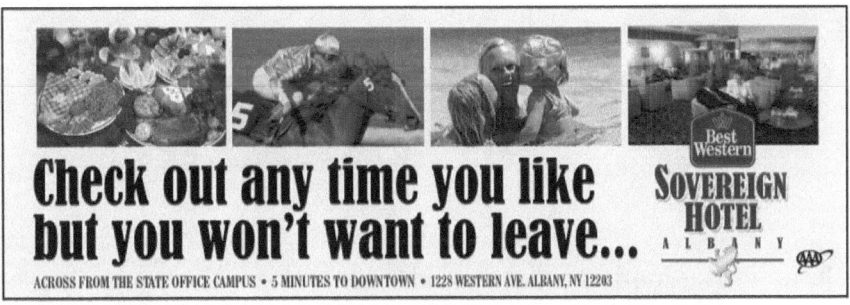

Amusing can work to command attention but as with every other example, it must be related to what you are selling.

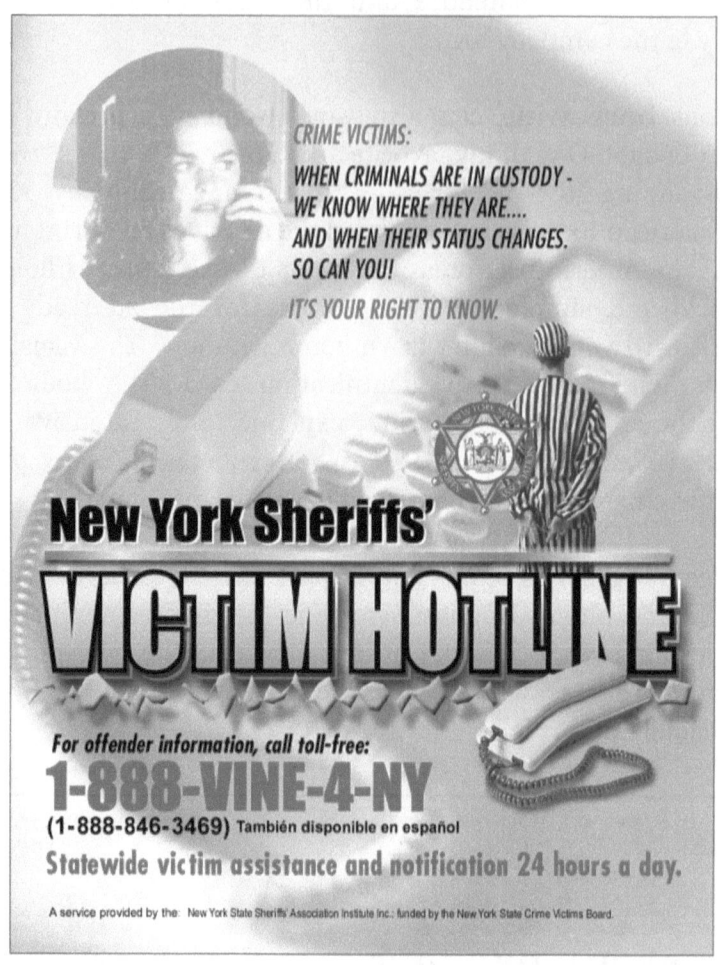

Fear is the motivator in this ad. The look on the woman's face shows her worry. The phone leads right from the headline to the Hotline number. If people are scared of something, they will pay attention.

If in doubt, *don't hesitate* to make the product the star of the ad. It is after all what you are selling.

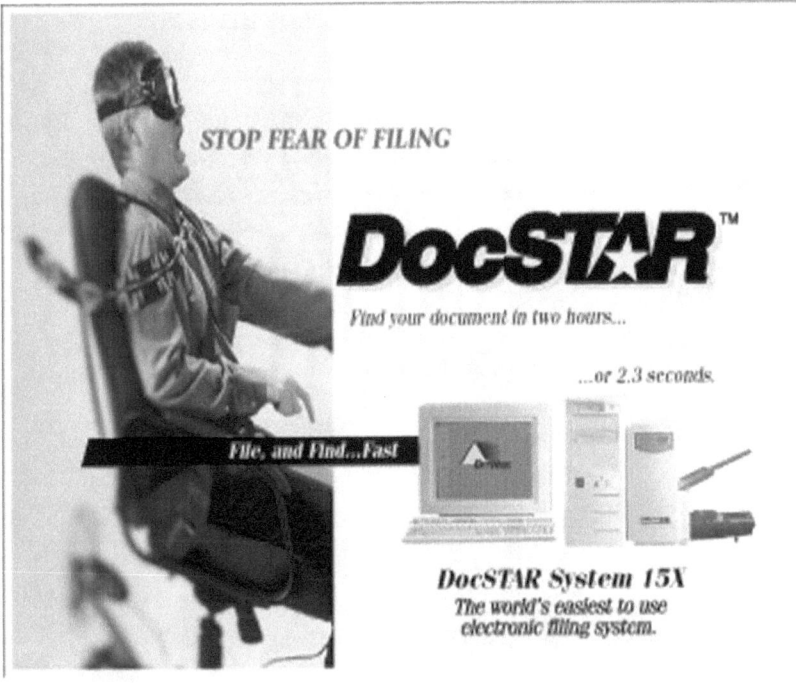

A word play on "fear of flying" and a visual that shows speed... *"find your document in two hours or in 2-3 seconds."* All graphics lead to the product!

Whenever possible show the *benefit* of it to the viewer. A holiday beach destination that looks irresistible. Food photos that the viewer salivates over. Products in use, services rendered, and causes worth supporting. Showing the product or service in use in a positive problem solving way is the best way to convince the viewer.

Last but not least, although for some reason designers instinctively rebel against using for "esthetic reasons" strong visuals and typography supporting: FREE *(the most effective word in the English language)* - SAVE MONEY - BIGGER -BETTER - NEW - IMPROVED - FASTER - GET MORE - LIMITED TIME

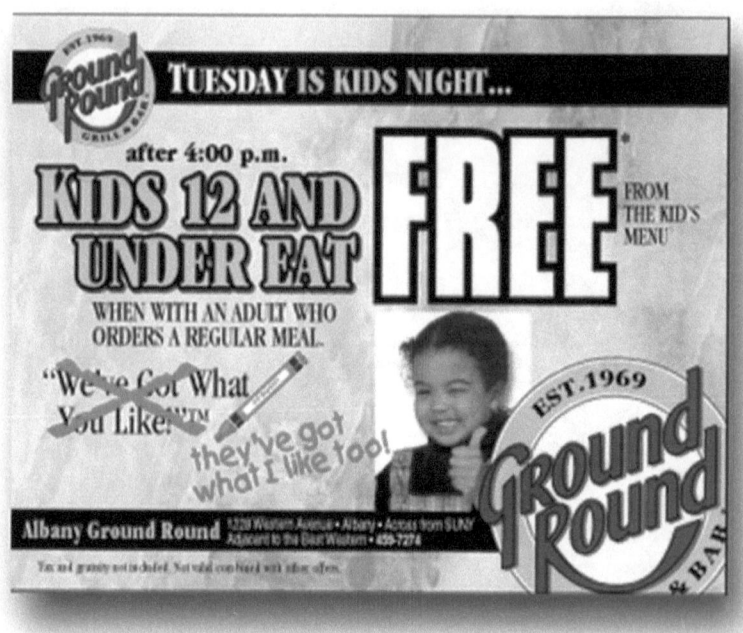

FREE is a powerful word and one of the best four letter words in the English language. The cute kid next to the Ground Round logo and address tells you who, what and where.

OFFER and the like, are effective and should be used large and bold. Ugly but time proven graphics like starbursts, bellybands or banners, in consumer understood colors like red and yellow work too. *Remember, we are not making art for the Guggenheim or the Louvre - we are in the business of selling and communicating a message.*

2.COMMUNICATE CLEARLY.

No room for artsy-trendy here. Art has nothing to do with good design. Copy, typography and graphics must be concise and clear. One strong visual image will usually have more impact and clarity than a page full of images. However, we always have to remember our audience. The below ad was aimed at bar and nightclub owners and managers who live in a visually hectic environment. The visuals reflect this BUT the product still stands out:

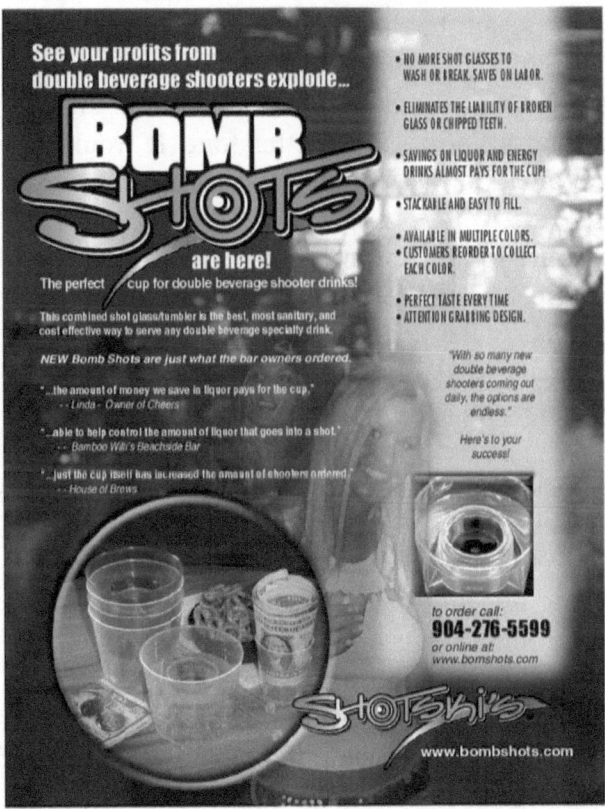

The color version of this is filled with day glow bright colors blending into a typically dark busy bar scene.

TYPOGRAPHY

There are countless typefaces (fonts) available today. There are serif, sans serif, scripts, gothic, decorative, black letter and a host of other styles. To my mind, they only fall into TWO categories:

1. Use for headlines.
2. Use for body text.

You can use anything you want for headlines and sub heads as long as they: A. Fit the theme of the design and B. Are readable!

Obviously, a script headline font makes more sense for a wedding store ad than a gothic block letter font. It would be very wrong though for an ad for heavy industrial equipment.

When it comes to text however, simple, common and readable text fonts are imperative. Preferably a serif face especially if the text is long. Classics like Times Roman, Garamond, Cheltenham, Baskerville and Palatino never go out of style and are very readable and legible.

For emphasis and brevity the use of • bulleted copy is best and especially good for benefits or features. I will use them here:
• Avoid long text in reverse (i.e. white or light color on dark or black backgrounds). It is impossible to read easily.
• Use as few different fonts as possible.
• Contrasting fonts works well. A mix of serif and sans serif breaks up messages into easily seen differences. Never mix different serif faces. – it just adds visual clutter.
• Value contrast (light vs. dark) eases readability.
• Color and chromatic contrast is equally important.

TYPOGRAPHY

Serif face samples:
Times Roman - Georgia - Palatino - Chaparral

Sans Serif samples:
Arial - **Franklin Gothic** - Tahoma - Myriad

Decorative/specialty samples:
STENCIL - *Script* - **BREWERS** - Bernhard

Set as a paragraph - note that the serif face is easier to read and the script version - almost imposible

Adam Barthold is a deeply flawed man haunted by the mysterious Arahm Tuit. He travels from upstate New York to the hills of Ash Fork, Arizona where he hopes to start a new life but instead finds love, danger and watches the world come tumbling down in red ruin, little knowing he has an important part to play in the future of human kind.

Adam Barthold is a deeply flawed man haunted by the mysterious Arahm Tuit. He travels from upstate New York to the hills of Ash Fork, Arizona where he hopes to start a new life but instead finds love, danger and watches the world come tumbling down in red ruin, little knowing he has an important part to play in the future of human kind.

Adam Barthold is a deeply flawed man haunted by the mysterious Arahm Tuit. He travels from upstate New York to the hills of Ash Fork, Arizona where he hopes to start a new life but instead finds love, danger and watches the world come tumbling down in red ruin, little knowing he has an important part to play in the future of human kind.

Condensed type saves space but is very hard to read -

Adam Barthold is a deeply flawed man haunted by the mysterious Arahm Tuit. He travels from upstate New York to the hills of Ash Fork, Arizona where he hopes to start a new life but instead finds love, danger and watches the world come tumbling down in red ruin, little knowing he has an important part to play in the future of human kind.

TYPOGRAPHY IN USE

Set in reverse is likewise - unwise - unless it is only a few words

Adam Barthold is a deeply flawed man haunted by the mysterious Arahm Tuit. He travels from upstate New York to the hills of Ash Fork, Arizona where he hopes to start a new life but instead finds love, danger and watches the world come tumbling down in red ruin, little knowing he has an important part to play in the future of human kind.

Set even larger, poor contrast and/or reverse text is HARD to read!

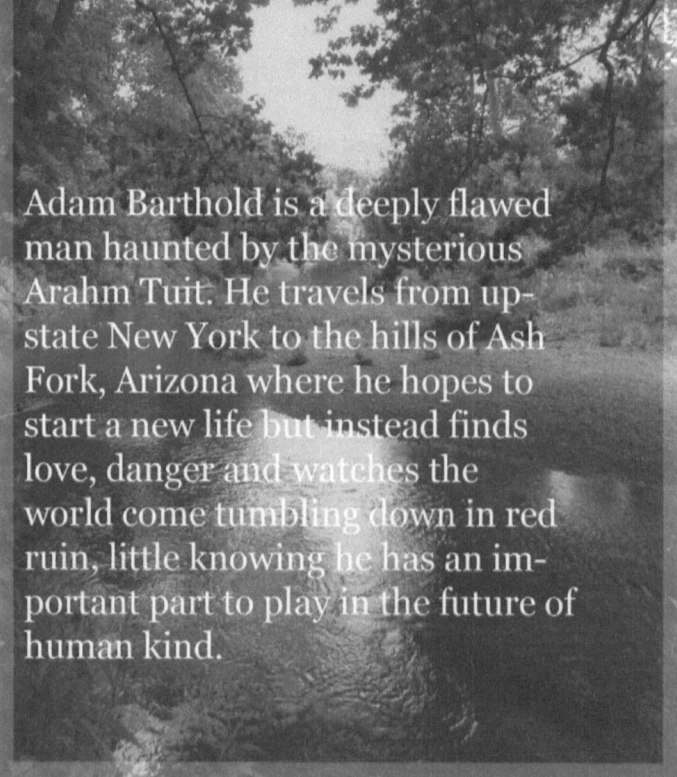

Adam Barthold is a deeply flawed man haunted by the mysterious Arahm Tuit. He travels from upstate New York to the hills of Ash Fork, Arizona where he hopes to start a new life but instead finds love, danger and watches the world come tumbling down in red ruin, little knowing he has an important part to play in the future of human kind.

I was designing a seafood package years ago that had a medium dark blue ocean scene in the background. I used yellow for the benefits and sales points so they would stand out. The client insisted on using red because "red will make the copy stand out." Despite my advice that the colors would clash, vibrate and be extremely hard to read, he wanted to see it. Fortunately, "seeing is believing" and we went back to yellow after he saw a proof.

• Make it big enough to read easily. Save the 6-point sans serif ultra-condensed for disclaimer or mandatory regulatory copy.

The temptation to cram the copy into an ad to make the most room for your incredibly clever and artistic graphic must be resisted - *Strongly*. The visual is to get the consumers attention but the copy is what sells.

• Keep line lengths to 5-8 words, anything longer fatigues the eye and makes the transition from the end of one line to the next difficult.

I was reviewing a two-fold 8 ½" x 11" brochure a friend and colleague of mine had just designed and noted she had used Belwe light (an artsy but unusual font) to the full measure across both folds. When I asked why she enthusiastically replied: "I like it!" Because we were friends and she once saved my ass big time, I kept quiet but nobody could or would want to read the thing. Liking something personally has nothing to do with form or function. We are not in the "liking what we like" business we are in the communication business.

• Italics are best used to *emphasize* a word within a line of text. Italics used in headlines push the reader's eye off to the right. That being said, if italic fonts are set at an angle upward they can have impact.

• When using all CAPS, it is best if the headline or subhead is brief. Long lines of capital letters are also hard to read.

• Don't labor at length over what font to use. Choose three to five fonts, view them together then choose one.

I had an employee once who spent an hour trying to decide on a font. She was blowing the budget and wasting time I was paying her for. I looked over her should at the screen and said: "just pick one and move on."

Even worse, the in house designer for a client of mine took a MONTH to choose a font for a new line of beverages. It was by the way a terrible choice. Pointed Brush, a very nice script but as it had to be set in an arch over the product vignette it looked weak and read terribly.

• Pursuant to the above comment, NEVER, EVER set a script in all CAPS... it simply is not designed to be used that way and it is impossible to read.

• Lastly, when in doubt: KISS off (Keep It Simple Stupid)

Be prepared however, to be asked the occasional question: "Do you think this is the right font for this ad?" Be prepared to respond to this question with a logical answer unless like me you are semi-retired and can reply: "actually I had no clue so I just picked something because I knew that you could fix it." In pre-computer times when clients and account executives were not constantly sitting at a keyboard composing amateur documents, they never even heard of the term "font." It was just the "lettering" to them so they rarely, if ever commented on the use of a particular typeface.

DESIGN: A.K.A. COMPOSITION

The layout of an ad or any other piece of graphic design for that matter needs to lead the viewer where you want them to go. The "flow" should ultimately lead them to the call for action. With stops along the way for the sales copy, supporting photos, graphics, illustrations, features and benefits. The samples on the following pages will illustrate this. Note when you view them, that the design is often simplified by using overlapping elements which visually tend to become only one element, hence reducing clutter. The position and facing of graphics lead mostly inward and downward bringing the viewer along and keeping their eye from wandering off the page and possibly to someone else's ad or something else of passing interest like their cup of coffee.

There are many ways of doing this. Some art directors swear by the Z format where all elements follow the visual direction of the letter "Z" until at the bottom right you reach the final destination: The all-important call to action. Others, like David Ogilvy and his followers, prefer an A layout where the eye catching visual is at the top of the page and all else falls into place directly below. The bottom line is that you may choose any way you wish to accomplish the purpose, BUT if you have a scattering of ill conceived, random elements roaming about the page with no rhyme or reason you will fail to communicate well.

Henri de Toulouse Lautrec was a 19th century painter of great renown but he was also an accomplished "commercial artist" in his day. Note the general Z pattern of the composition of this poster that begins at the eyes of the cat, down his body embracing Tournee du Chat Noir to the and tail which ends at the name Rodolptte Salis which is aided by the rectangle the cat sits on.

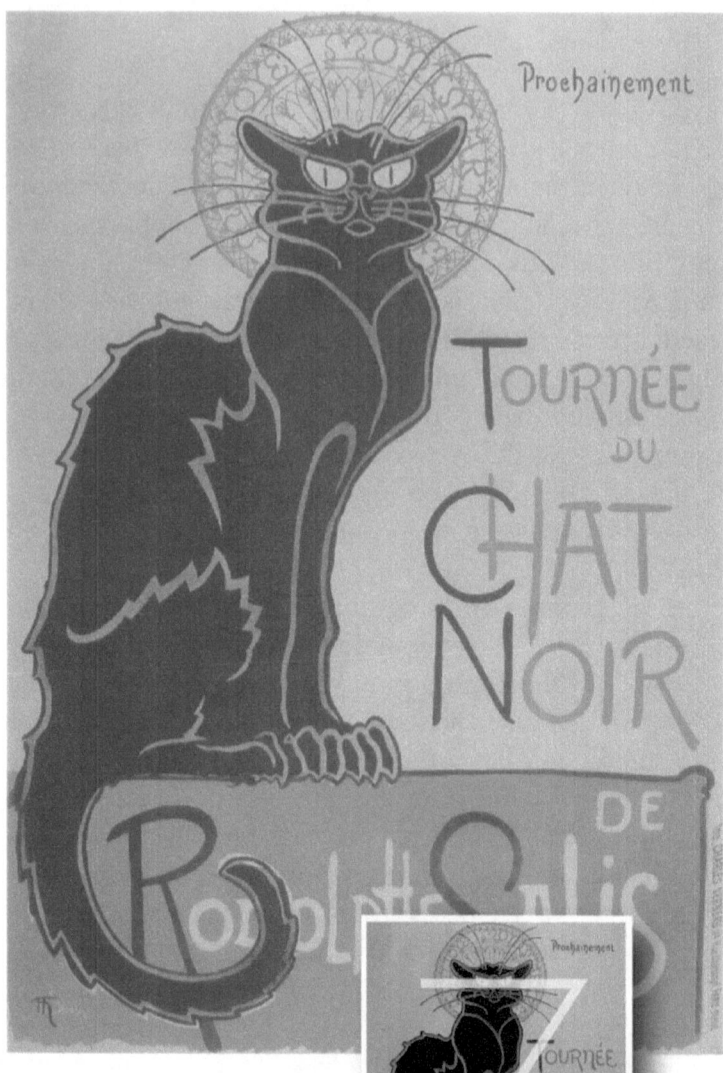

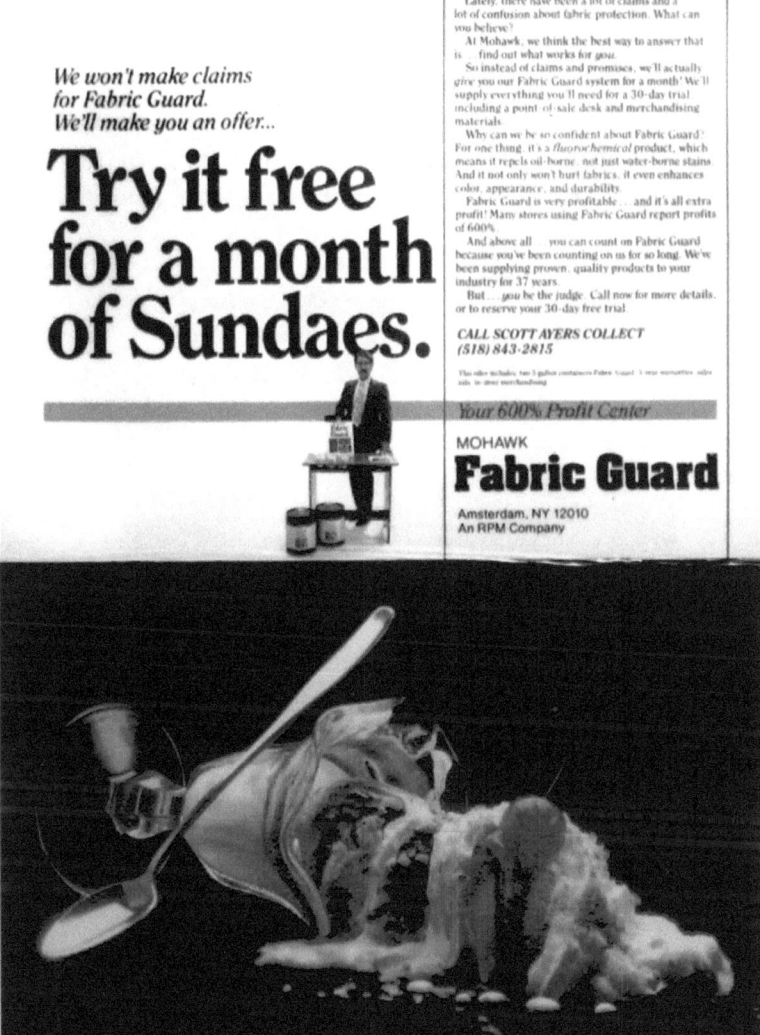

This ad is almost a classic "A layout" with the exception that the main photo is on the bottom. My double meaning pun headline underlaps the sales representative with the products and adjoins the call to action text. The spoon in the photo of the product in action repelling the spilled ice cream points back up to the product name and call to action.

3. MOTIVATE RESPONSE

Order today! Stop by the store! BUY me. Clip the coupon! Go to our web site! Call our 800 number! E-mail us for more information! The goal of most marketing communication is to sell a product or service. **Make it easy!** Note the Z pattern of the layout. The ultimate destination is number 3 – the coupon.

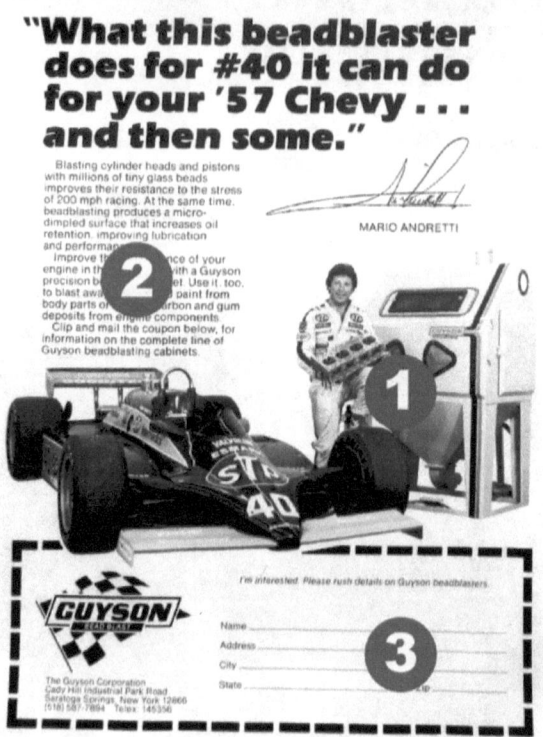

Legendary racer car driver Mario Andretti (1.) and one of his cars standing next to the product. The quote by Andretti was real. 2. Body copy explains the technical and manufacturing benefits. 3. Response coupon *that today would probably be replaced by a website address, e-mail and toll free phone number.*

Of the three there is a definite PRIMARY, SECONDARY AND TERTIARY priority emphasis as related to size, impact and importance. Organize the design in this way.

The 1-2-3 concept in practice:
The following examples illustrate the

Primary emphasis:
1. GET ATTENTION.
Secondary emphasis:
2. COMMUNICATE CLEARLY
Tertiary emphasis:
3. CALL TO ACTION – Motivate a response

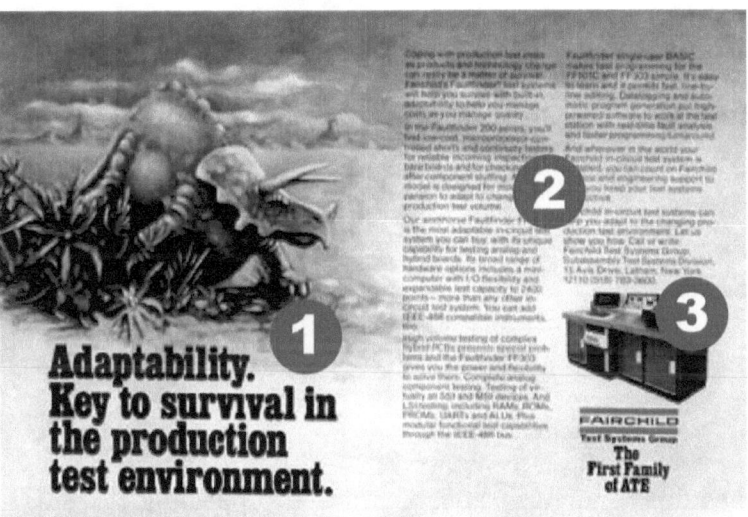

1. The headline and illustration.
2. The necessary long text explains the technical
and manufacturing benefits.
3. Product (facing into the text) and contact information.

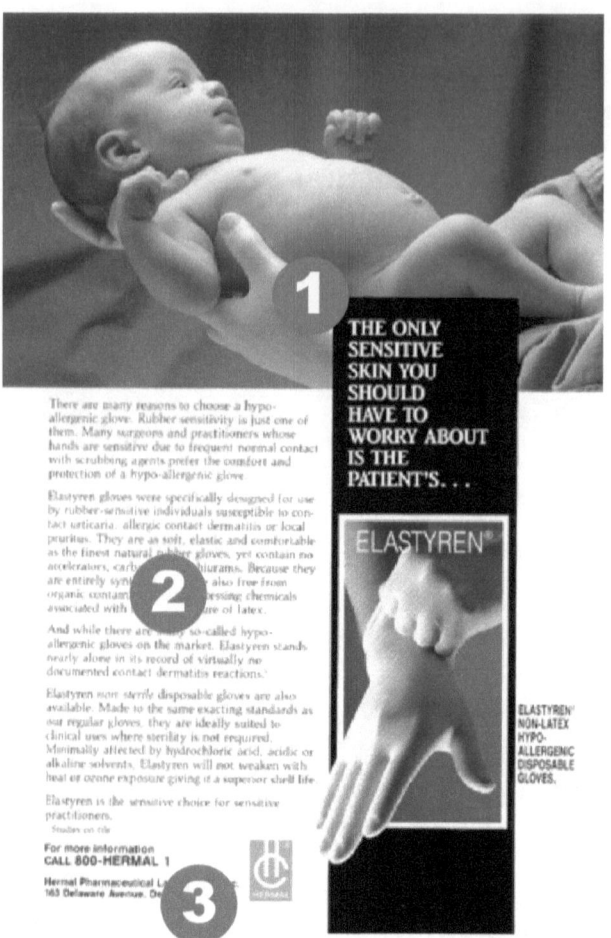

1. The headline and illustration feature an appealing infant. *(It was my youngest son at the time.)* The ad was written and designed to use a similar stock photo but was cost-prohibitive so he got his first and last modelling assignment. The hand model was me. His mother only trusted me to hold the kid.) 2. The necessary long text explains the hypoallergenic benefits to health care providers. 3. Company, product and contact information. Note that the hand directs the eye to this information.

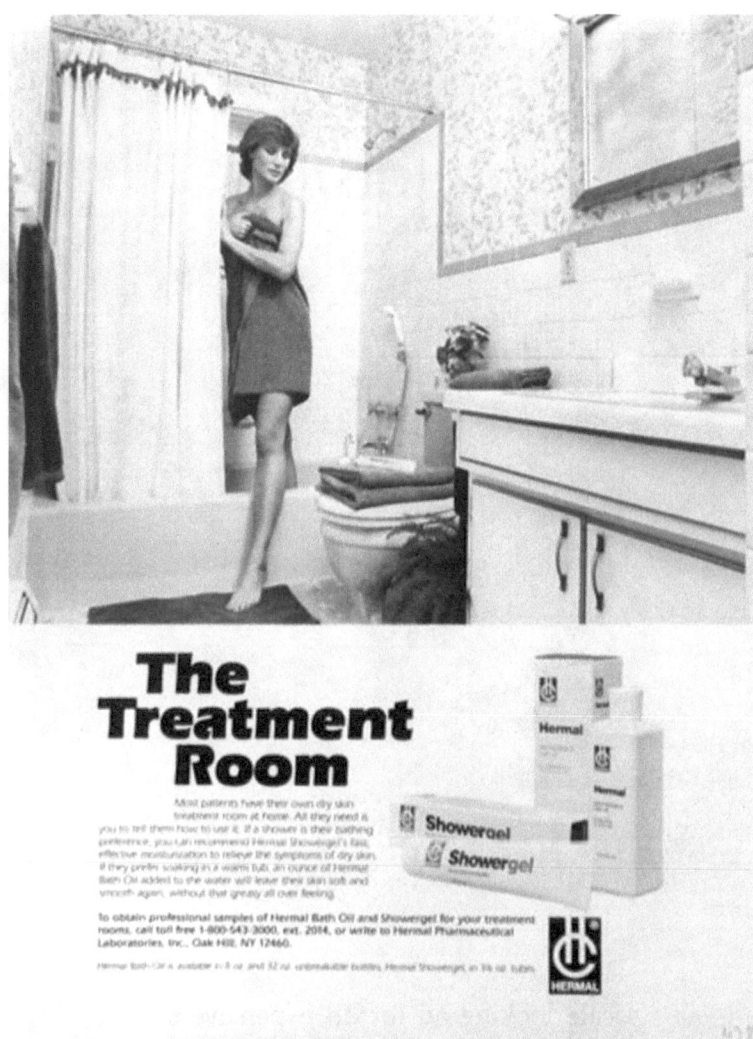

This is a good sample of an A layout. A large photo is on top of the page with the headline, body copy and call for action directly below. The product that was an ethical* dermatological treatment for dry skin is prominently featured.

*Ethical in this case it is marketed primarily by a doctor's recommendation.

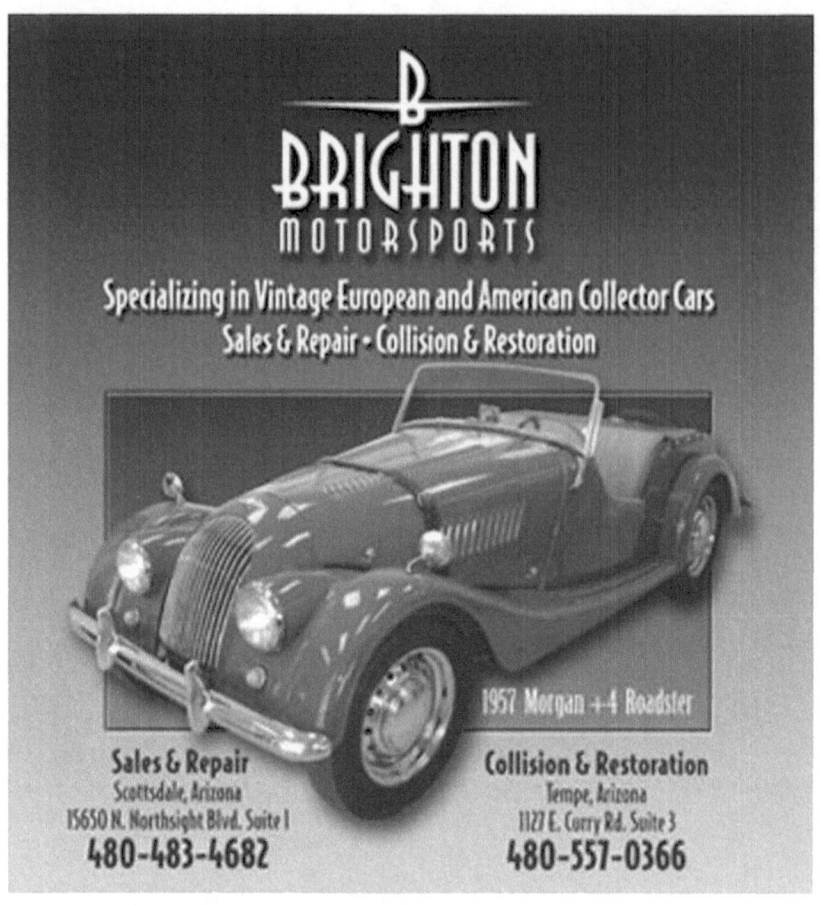

Brighton Motorsports

Specializing in Vintage European and American Collector Cars
Sales & Repair • Collision & Restoration

1957 Morgan +4 Roadster

Sales & Repair
Scottsdale, Arizona
15650 N. Northsight Blvd. Suite 1
480-483-4682

Collision & Restoration
Tempe, Arizona
1127 E. Curry Rd. Suite 3
480-557-0366

This is an upscale looking ad for an expensive service. Brighton did not do restoration and repair for your Dodge Neon or old bucket of bolts as you can tell by the photo of the car in the ad. In color, it is a bright red vehicle against a black background fading to charcoal gray to highlight the color.

http://www.creativecolleagues.com/advertising.htm

Outdoor Advertising: (i.e. billboards)

Despite that I consider outdoor boards to a visual blight on the landscape, they are a fact of life and not likely to be outlawed any time soon. With that in mind, there are some very operative considerations when designing them:

• Keep it **k.i.S.s.** – Keep it **SUPER** simple. Typically, unless the viewer is stuck in a traffic jam they have at best 3 seconds to see it and take in the message. Simple large visuals and three to five words in the headline supported by equally brief supporting text.

• Don't bother with phone numbers *unless* easily remembered. For example: 1-800-MADD (Mothers Against Drunk Drivers). Hopefully, nobody is going to try to jot down the number while navigating the highway – *hopefully*.

• Addresses are equally not needed *unless* it is something directional like: "3 miles ahead at exit 222" or "just ahead on your right."

• Be sure the headline is large and readable from a distance and in an easily read font. Billboards are no place for some artsy-fartsy new age typeface.

• Always, try to tie in the visual theme with other advertising or collateral graphics already in use.

This is an example of an outdoor board that supported an existing ad campaign:

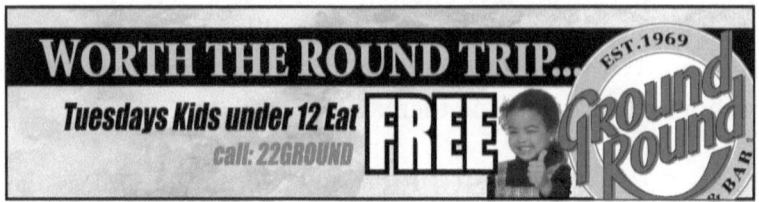

Billboard

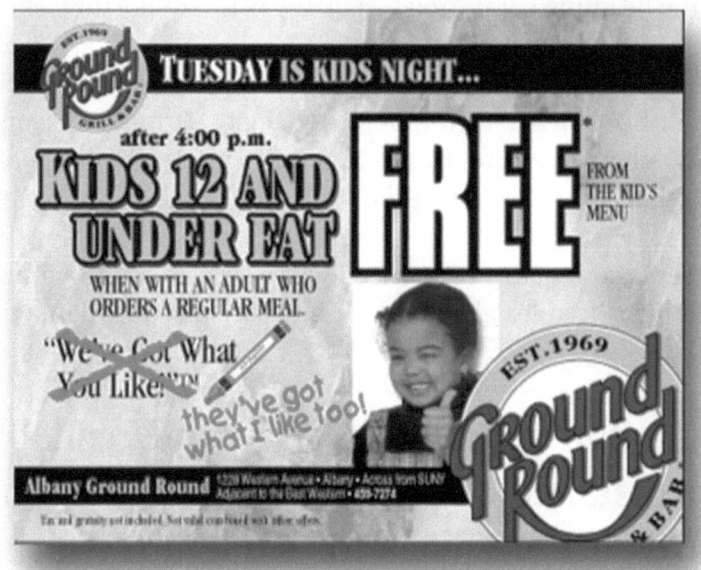

Print ad

A four word bold headline with pun intended leads directly to the logo supported by the cute child and the word FREE. The phone number (22GROUND) is easily remembered.

Note that it uses all the same elements and visual theme as the ad for the same offer. The little details including the address, disclaimers, additional cute support like the crayon and "they've got what I like too" copy have been omitted.

Direct Response and Directory Advertising

Very early in my career I made the mistake of using the term "junk mail" to my employer at D.J. Moore Advertising. With a firm but fatherly tone, he responded: "Son, we refer to that as direct response advertising. Remember that please."

Direct response advertising encompasses a large field from direct mail printed pieces including the value coupon packets that arrive in your mailbox, to the door hangers left at your doorstep, to the inevitable "spam" that winds up in your inbox on your computer, tablet or phone. Much of it targeted by the use of purchased mailing lists, selected zip codes or information gleaned from the internet and social media sites. And much of it finds its way to the "circular file" or encounters the delete button. This is well understood by the marketers and advertisers and accepted because it is a numbers game. More crudely put, "if you throw enough shit against the wall, some of it will stick." If the advertiser gets 2% of it to stick, meaning getting a response: *that is a success.* Anything above that is gravy. The response can be anything from generating a sales lead, getting an inquiry via phone or e-mail, to making a direct sale.

Our job as designers is to at least get to the success level or above and if we are lucky, we get to hit a home run or two in our careers. Much of the previously mentioned design advice for print media advertising design applies to direct response *but with some important differences.*

Unlike print media, we often have either very small spaces to deal with or larger formats with two sides or multiple pages. Often some of this space is taken up by legal disclaimers or marketing caveats like expiration dates, exclusions and other "fine print gotcha's." Regardless, we still have *to command attention, clearly communicate and motivate response.* Often this has to be done for multiple products or services, special offers and auxiliary products.

These small space pieces require tight organization and a shoehorn at times. The larger multiple page pieces require discipline to not waste space and in some cases to relegate some information to the black and white side for the sake of economy in printing. In addition to this, unlike most general advertising they often need to list every damn service and product the company offers and detailed multiple response options. *This is important!* Many times consumers look for the details. In this case, these mailers are just like the old-fashioned yellow pages ads. *For example*, one-day year's back, I was looking for a company to service my water softener unit. My decision as to who I was first to call was made when I saw my brand (Kinetico) listed in their ad. Being the first called increases the chance of making a sale tenfold or more. So even though the "inner artist" in you rebels about the clutter – it is your job to unclutter it and organize it to communicate and sell effectively.

Phone directory ads are disappearing fast because search engines like Google, have replaced printed telephone directories. They have mostly become the "buggy whips" of modern times. Today, with web pages, Facebook and a variety of other computer media advertising making use of small spaces is even more important than ever. And more competitive.

The following pages show some examples of direct mail and directory ads.

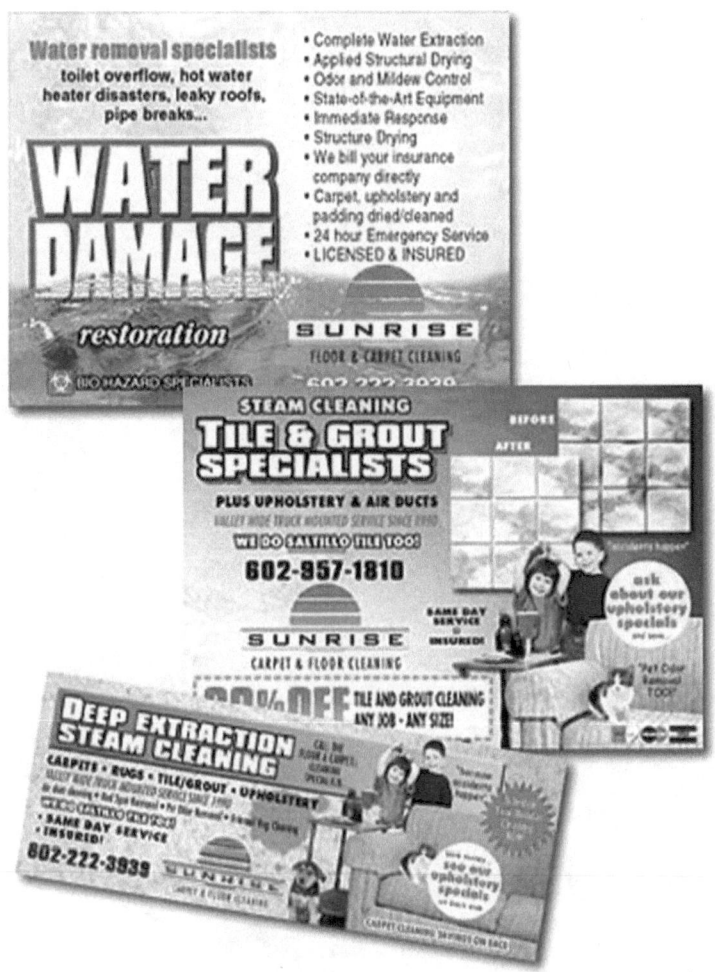

These were directory/mailer ads, also Val-Pak Mailer inserts. Each had a main service emphasis but also cross-referenced other services offered, special pricing, coupon savings, payment options, licensing information, phone numbers and many other options available to their customers. All were 4" x 6" or less.

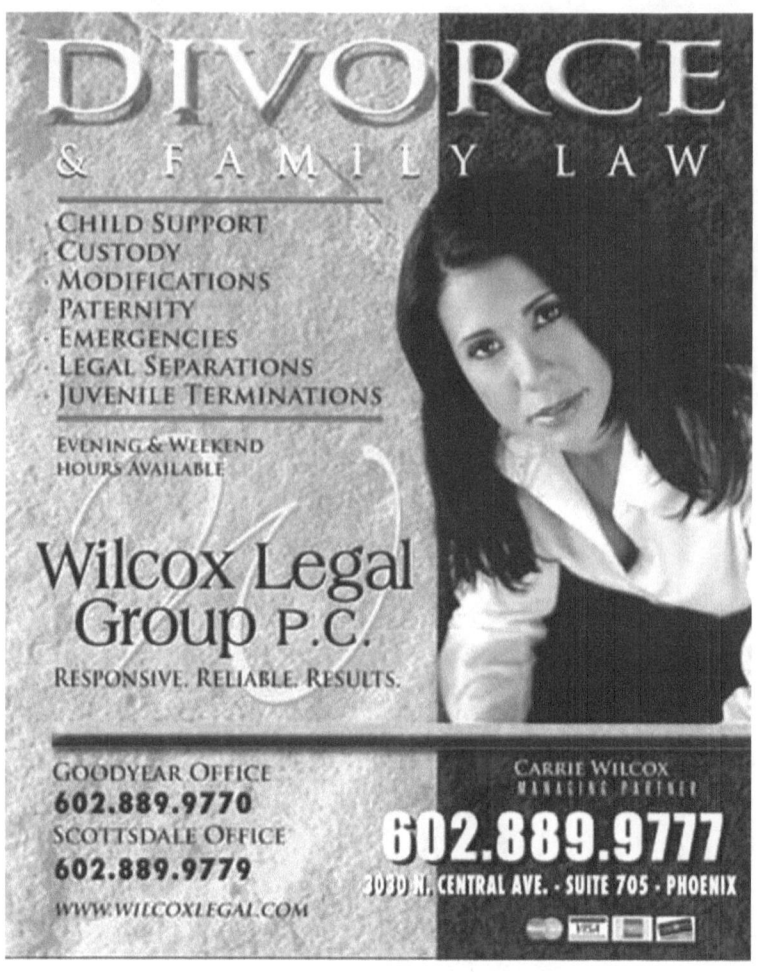
This large directory ad lists all forms of legal services handled by the firm, card services accepted, multiple locations, hours and website information. Their specialty was divorce and family law hence the large headline. The photo of the attractive managing partner looking right at you rivets the viewer's attention and leans into the ad. The general look of the ad is very professional but with a feminine touch because the managing partner was a woman.

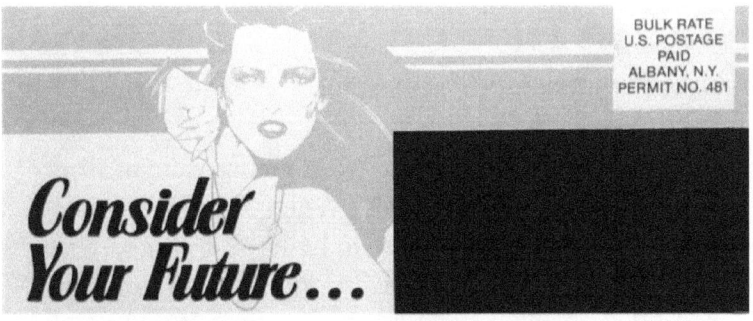

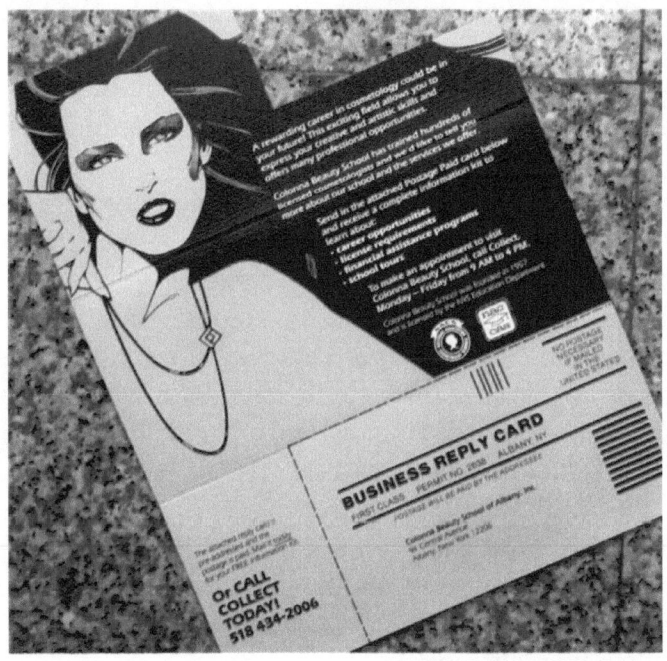

Sometimes you hit a home run. In this case, it was out of the park. This was aimed at young women to get them to consider enrolling at Colonna Beauty School. The top shows the mailer folded. The dark space next to headline was where the recipients mailing label was attached. Below it, the inside made the sales pitch. Because the die-cut and perforated response card required no effort other than tearing it off and dropping in the nearest mailbox our client got a **14% response rate!** *It also received a design award but the real reward was the response rate!*

Graphic Design
A much-misunderstood profession.

In my ill-spent youth, I once invited a young woman to my place with admittedly ulterior motives. When the early conversation turned to "what do you do for a living?" I thought the most expedient explanation would be to show her a portfolio of my work. I flipped through page after page, explaining some of the pieces, and what they were for, but when I finished she inquired: "But what do *you* do? Don't you just call a printer and have this stuff 'printed up'?" She was no dummy and in fact was a well-educated, professional nurse practitioner. I was dumbfounded.

Explaining the process and my part in it from designing (deciding what goes where and why), writing, drawing illustrations and graphics, selecting and/or art directing and retouching photographs, meeting with clients or account executives, making revisions, organizing it all, prepping the art for a printer, and checking proofs, took some time. Eventually my ulterior motives came to fruition, but realizing that most people have no idea what a graphic designer does came as a surprise to me. It still does.

PLEASE NOTE: All of the examples in this book are reproduced in black and white because of the budget constrictions of "print on demand" paperback books. *If you want to see, color renditions and much more please visit:*
www.creativecolleagues.com. Feel free to use the e-mail link buttons judiciously if you have questions. *If you have, ulterior motives* keep in mind that I am 63 and happily married!

I will break down this chapter into the following sub categories:

• Collateral
Printed pieces that are not media advertising including brochures, posters, sell sheets and point of purchase displays.

• Package Design
Graphics applies to packaging – not necessarily the industrial design structure.

• Web design
This will include business to business, individual and consumer sites.

• Logo Design
Also known grandiosely, as corporate identity.

Much like the design precepts of the previous chapter, these still have *to command attention, clearly communicate and motivate response although the response is not often the same.* The response for most of the above is less direct. Instead of asking for a call or an e-mail, it is mostly to build awareness, enhance image, inform in detail and in the case of packaging the response desired is to *purchase the product right now* as you see it on the shelf!

Note: As I spent the majority of my later career in package design, especially food and beverages, you will see that even the other categories reflect that fact.

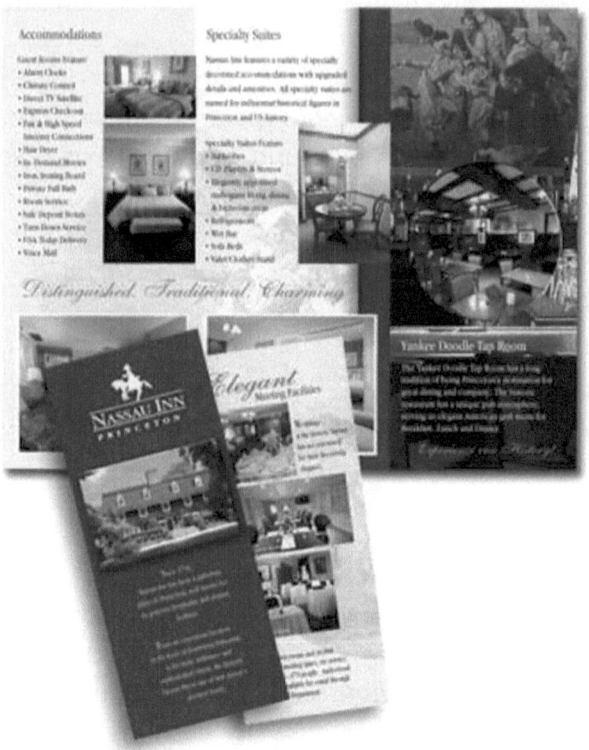

Collateral: Brochures

In the Beginning... man made the pamphlet. Other older terms included broadside, leaflet and flyer. The term brochure covers a broad spectrum of printed informational publications intended to inform, sell, convince or explain myriad people, places and things. Unless you are a newborn or a Himalayan Sherpa, you have seen and read countless numbers of these ubiquitous creations in countless sizes, shapes, with various numbers of pages and forms in your life.

The photo above is a typical two fold, six-panel piece for an elegant hotel in New Jersey.

The audience and purpose drives the design of each type. Commercial, consumer, public service, legal and financial brochures have different purposes and therefore demand different approaches but the 1-2-3 approach to design explained earlier still applies.

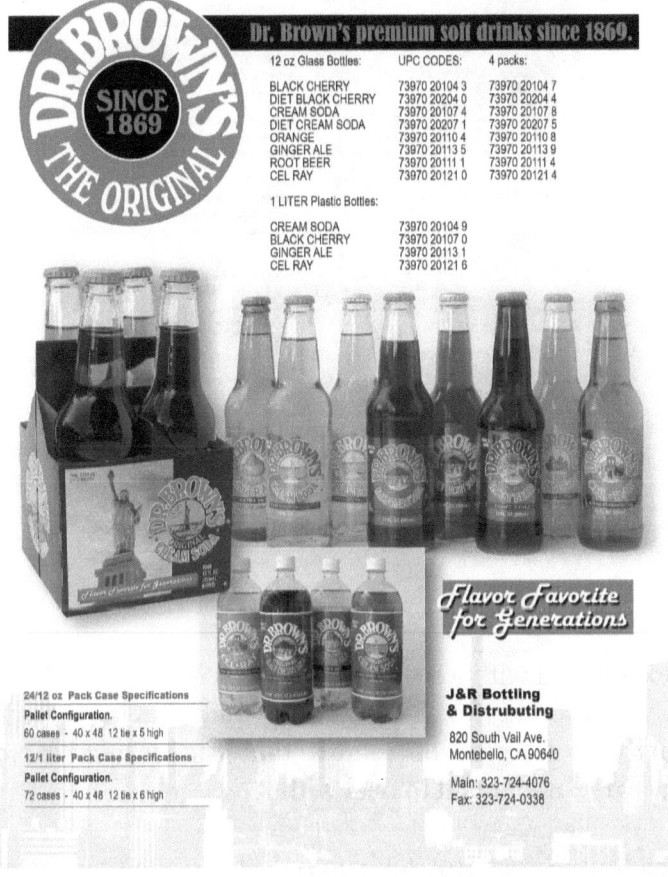

Above is a sales sheet for Dr. Brown's soda with specific information needed by beverage category buyers.

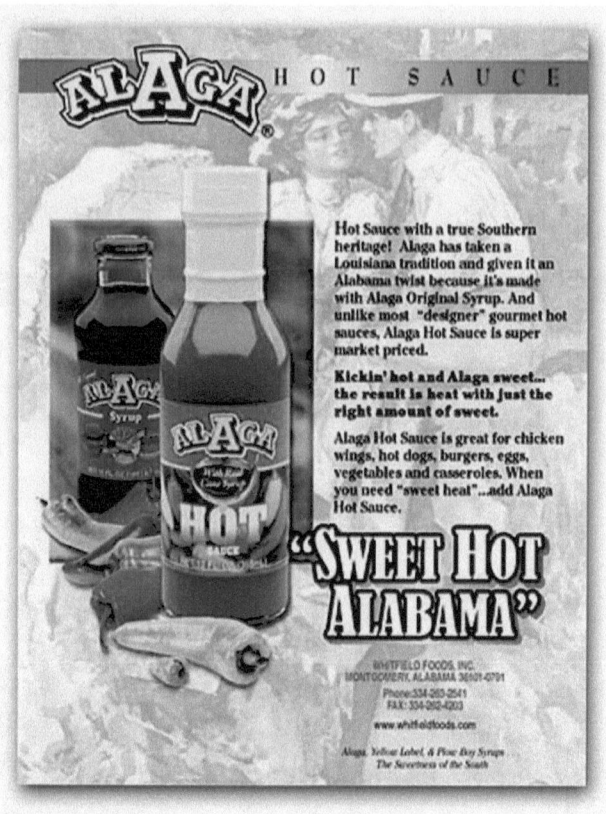

How do you deal with a really old and ugly package and logo? This brand was around for a long time and the logo represented Alabama and Georgia the states that the owners came from. Nobody cared BUT I had to deal with it.

The Headline 'Sweet Hot Alabama" a play on the movie and song title "Sweet Home Alabama" along with the vintage illustration in the background helped pull this together while still clearly showing the package. The peppers were stock images - added as accents to bring together two different products.

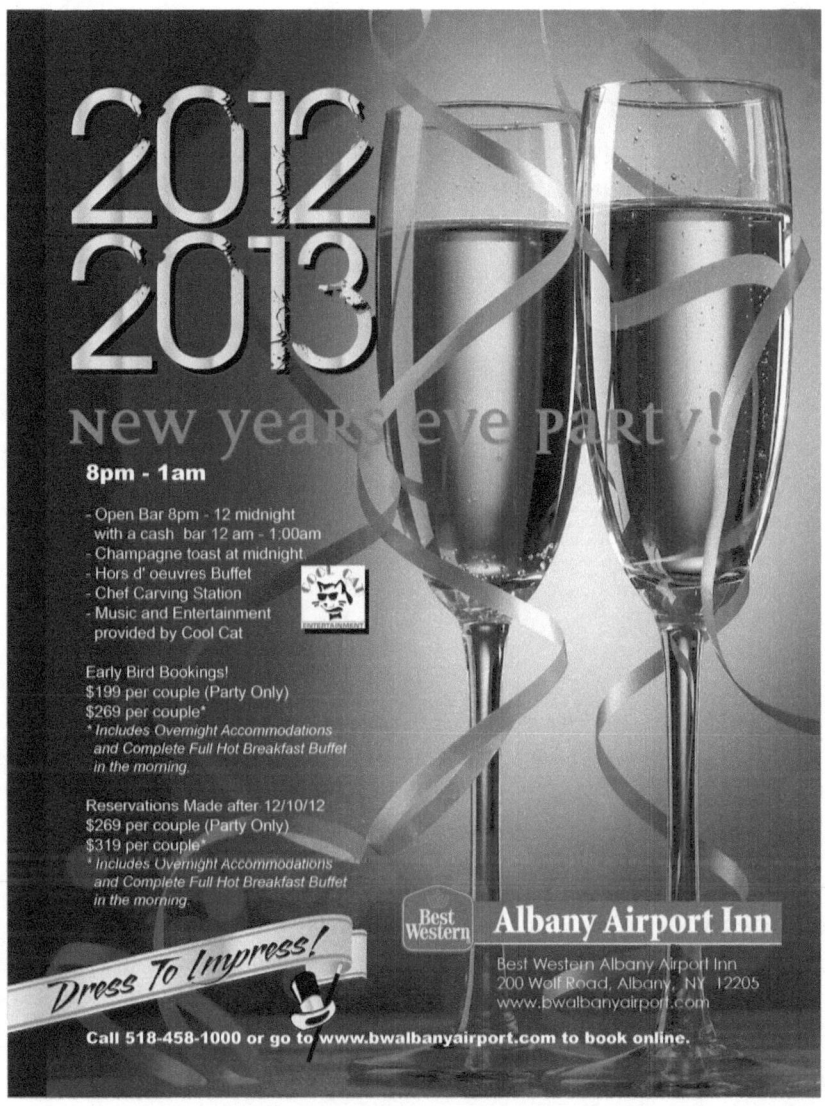

Above is a sales flyer for an upscale event at a hotel.
Note the details included without distracting from
the eye-catching photo.

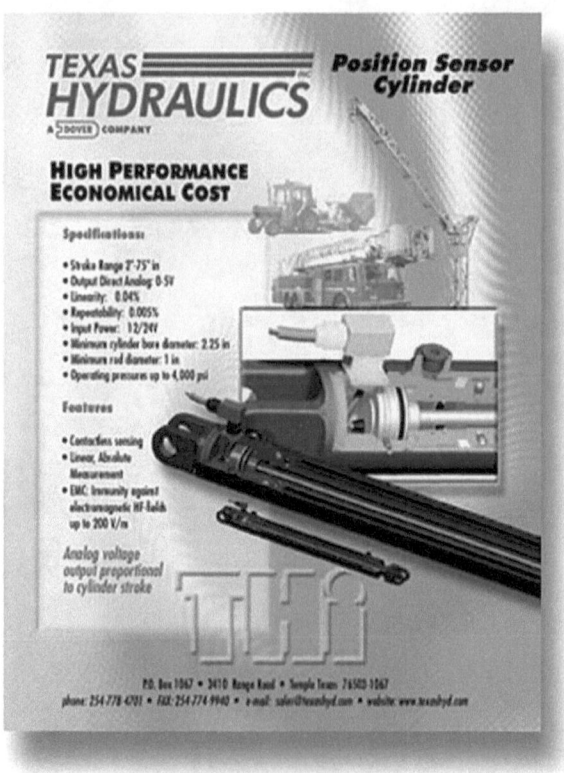

This is typical of an industrial brochure done for the lead engineer about a product that the general public would never see or even be interested in seeing but this is a large segment of the business-to-business graphic design world. While the close-up photos show the actual product, the small photos above are typical of the heavy machines it is used in. Because this was aimed at other design engineers, the specifications and features were important to show BUT the main heading summarizes the benefit:

High Performance - Economical Cost

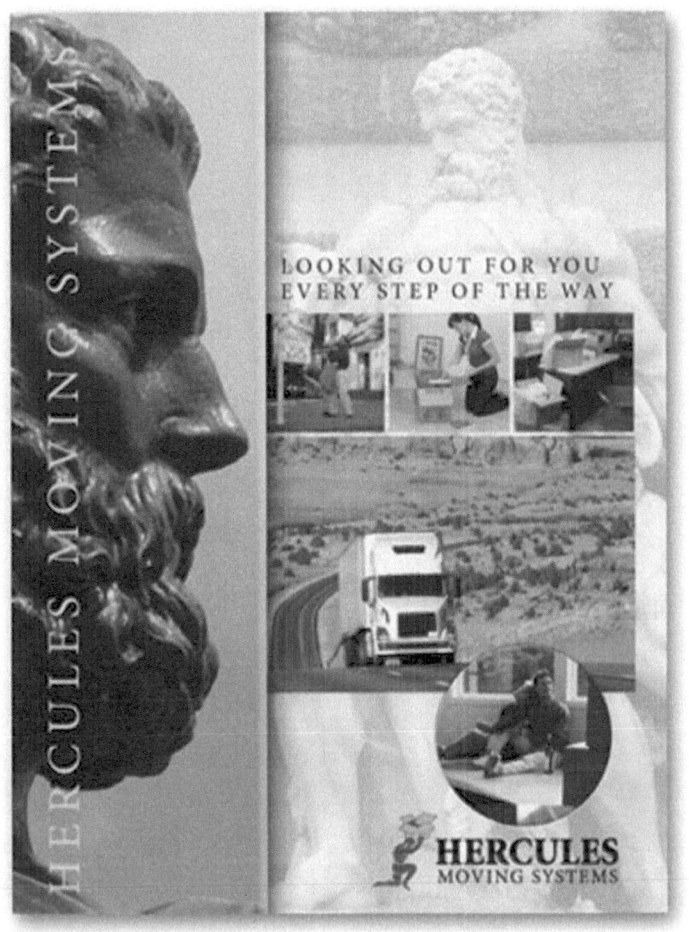

This brochure used the strong classic image of Hercules as a backdrop to the inset photos that literally showed moving from the for sale sign, to packing, the moving truck and final destination with the happy but tired couple ready to unpack.

Note: Since this company was affiliated with Nationwide previously shown in, advertising the same photo was used.

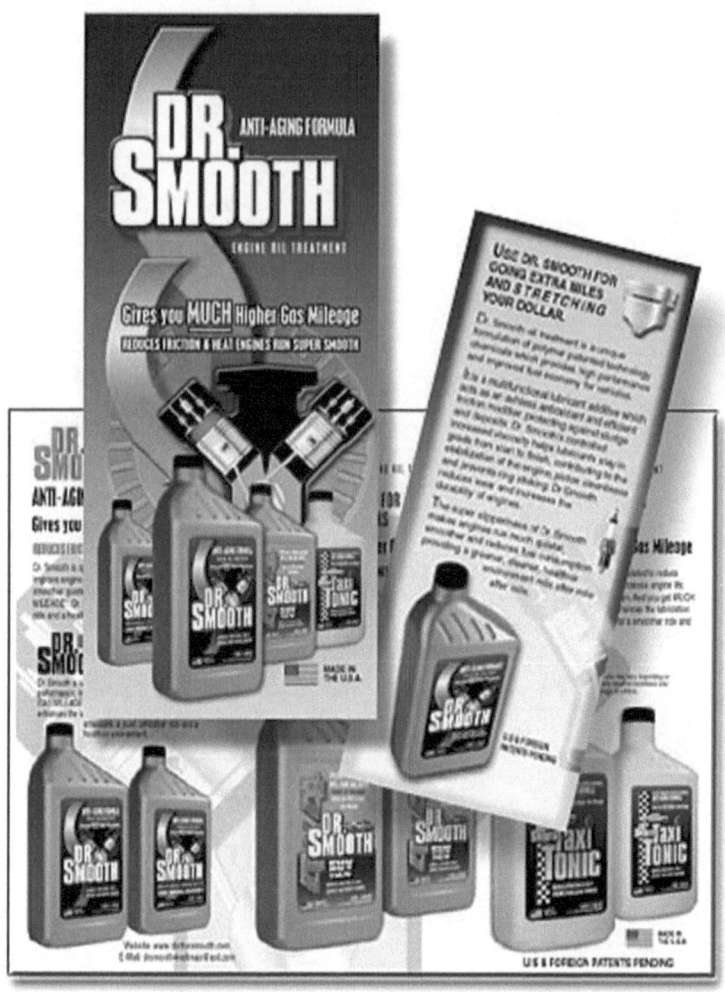

This 2-fold brochure features four products but the cover focused on their flagship product and its primary benefit of giving the consumer "MUCH higher gas mileage." The stylized "S" from the labels brings the viewer's eye down through the benefit sub head to the piston illustration to the product photos.

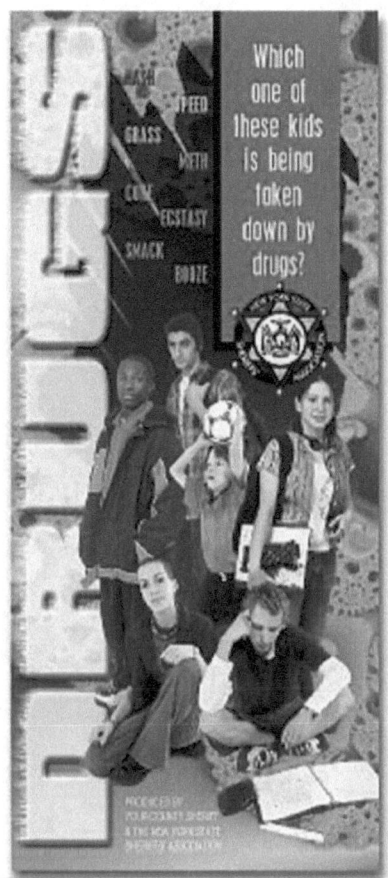

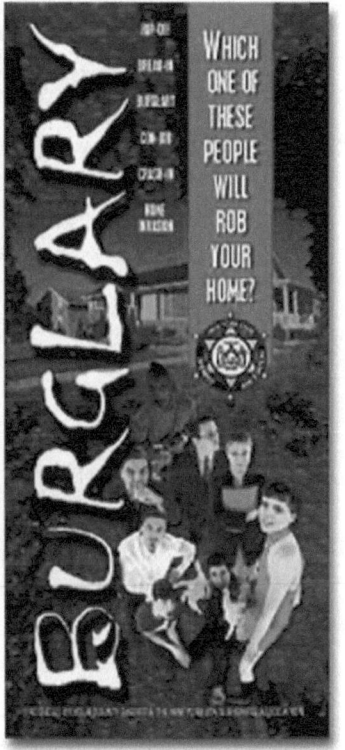

These were a series of public service brochures for the New York State Sheriffs' Association. The headline asks a provocative question that the inside explains in detail. The font and photos are different but the vertical bar and logo, relate them together in series.

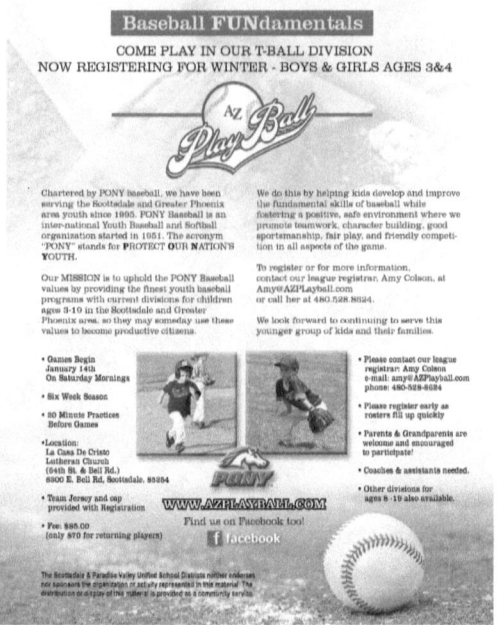

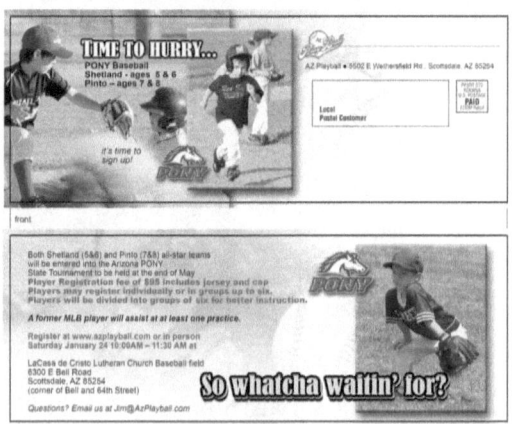

Volunteer design work for a baseball league I coached in for 12 years.
Note that the flyer and mailer share similar graphics for continuity.

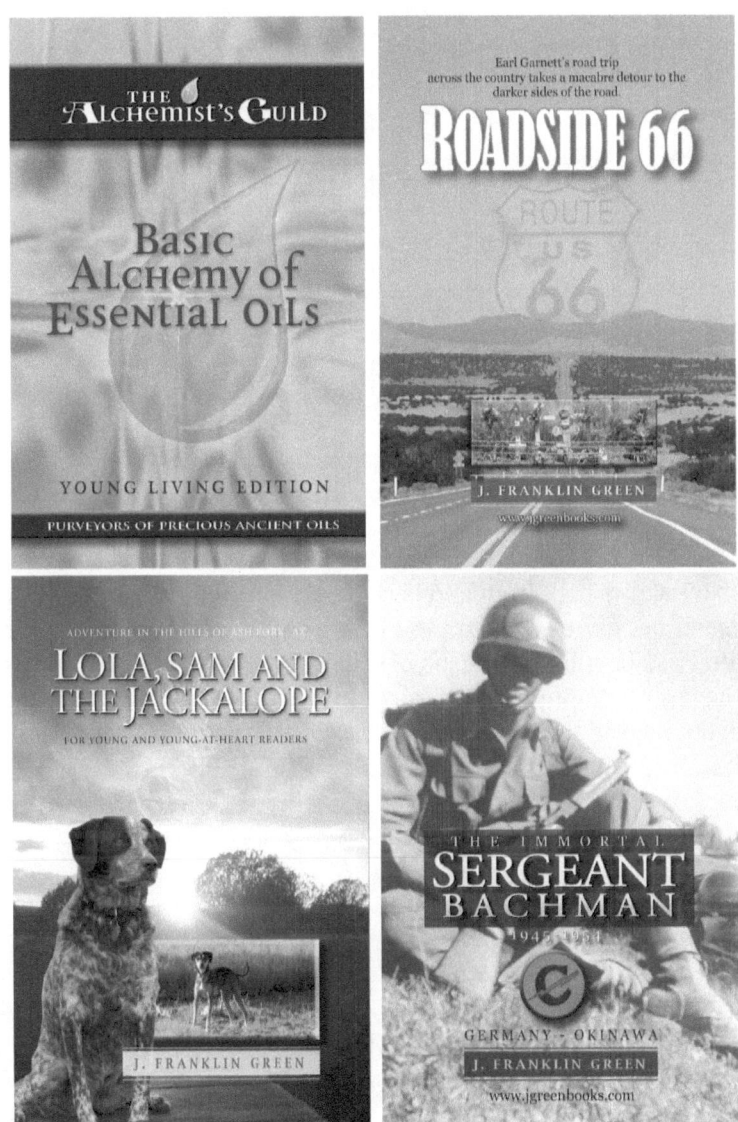

Book cover designs. Note the clarity of typography. Often these appear on websites the size of postage stamps. Readability as well as graphics is crucial, including title and author.

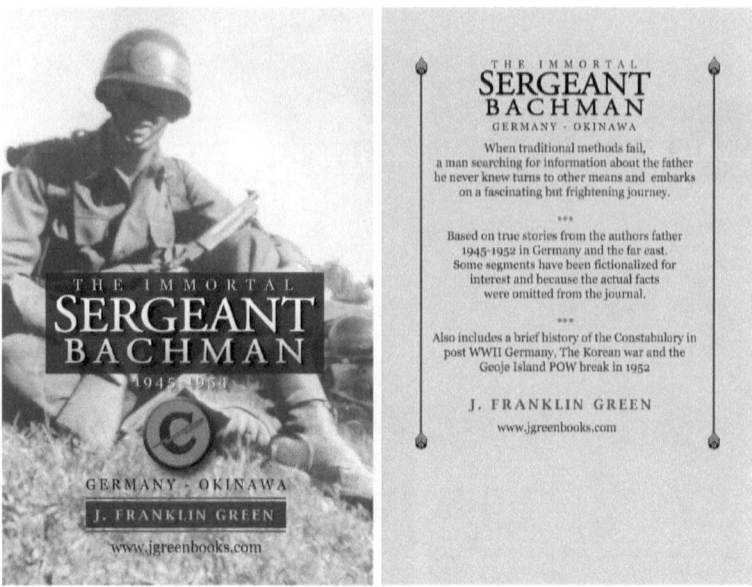

The above shows both front and back cover. The descriptions on the back are sometimes more important than the front cover. The synopsis for potential readers finishes the job of selling the book. Below cover was also the basis of their package design. In this case, the author is not noted, but instead the company - *The Alchemist's Guild*.

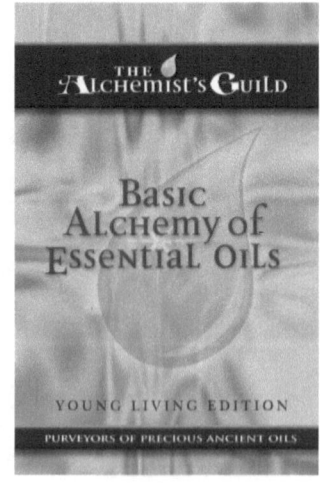

Collateral: Point of Purchase

As the name implies, this form of collateral advertising is also known as Point-Of-Sale, to be placed near or directly adjacent to the product or business. The purpose is to call attention to the product and help sell it. This type includes posters, static clings, shelf talkers or danglers, floor decals, signs, channel strips, table tents and banners. I prefer the term Point Of Purchase because the common acronym for it is POP as opposed to POS a well, known acronym and the type of design we like to avoid. The number one job of POP is to POP. The design and message need to *pop* off the shelf, or off the store window or wall. Sometimes that job is simply to attract attention to a product already on the shelf *and often directly adjacent to that of a competitor at the supermarket,* add a benefit oriented sales message or a superior price or value point. Many times as in the case of posters and banners, the purpose is to direct the consumer to new products, specially priced existing products or products that are outside the normal offerings. And yes, the design as always needs to follow the 1-2-3 method albeit sometimes in truncated form.

Posters:

For years, I designed store posters for a medium sized submarine sandwich chain in upstate New York named Mr. Subb. The designs always had a visually continuous theme but called attention to new menu options, or special value deals on existing products. In addition to the appetizing product photos, I used humorous cartoon characters and take offs on songs to draw the viewer into the message. For example: "Baby it's cold outside..." (a fraction of a popular song lyric), so come in and order a hot Subb! In each case, the goofy guy with the guitar belted out lyrics related to the product offering.

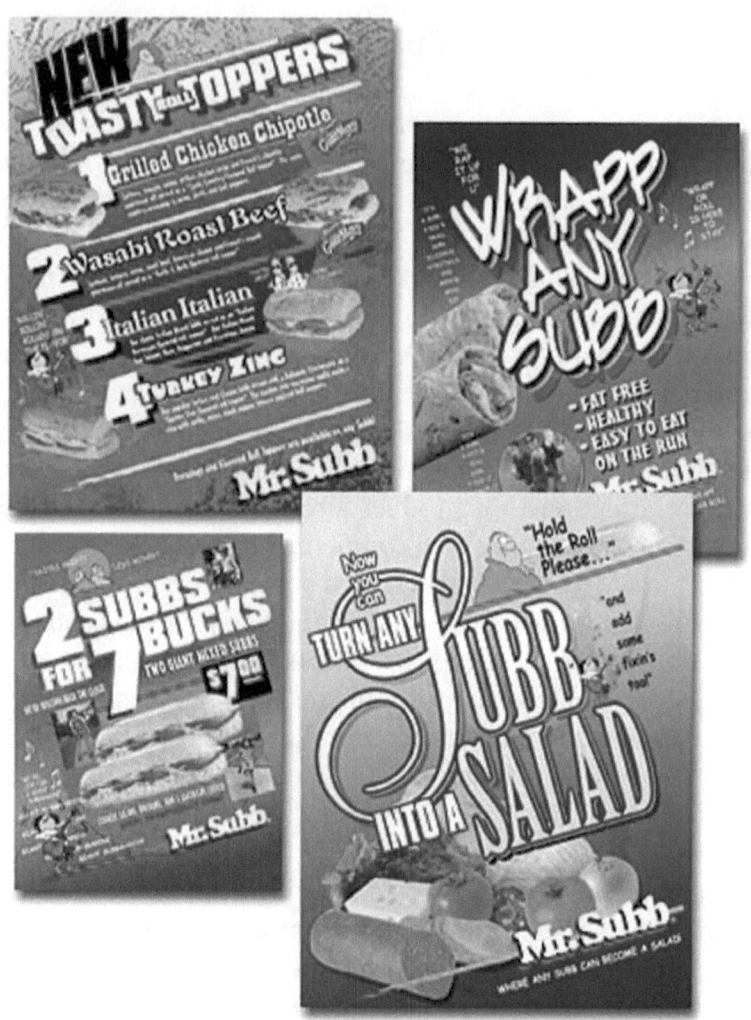

Unlike billboards, people have time to read store posters while waiting outside for companions to arrive, waiting to order or even while eating their current order and perhaps induce them to come back and try something else the next time. The marketing manager and the CEO loved them *and so did their customers*. And most importantly, they increased sales!

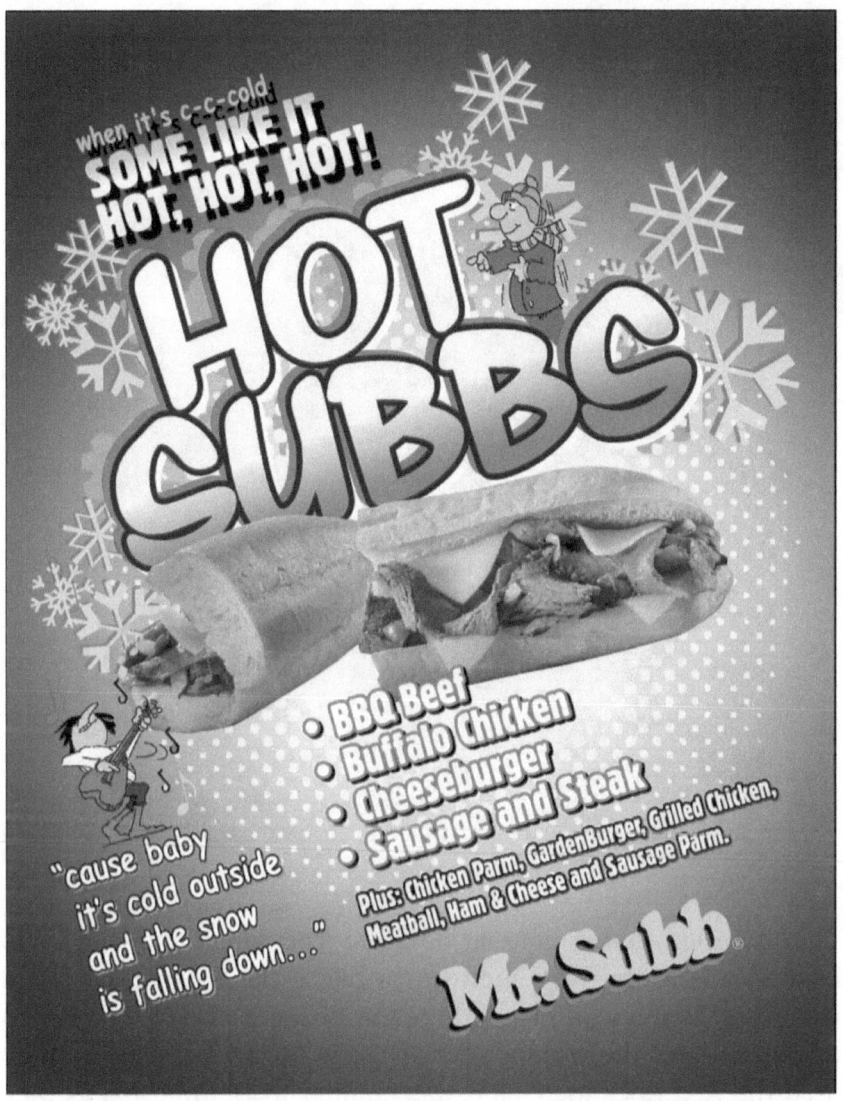

These posters were very large format often filling an entire widow panel at the stores. The headline like the one above was easily read from the parking lot but also had lots of information and fun as customers got closer.

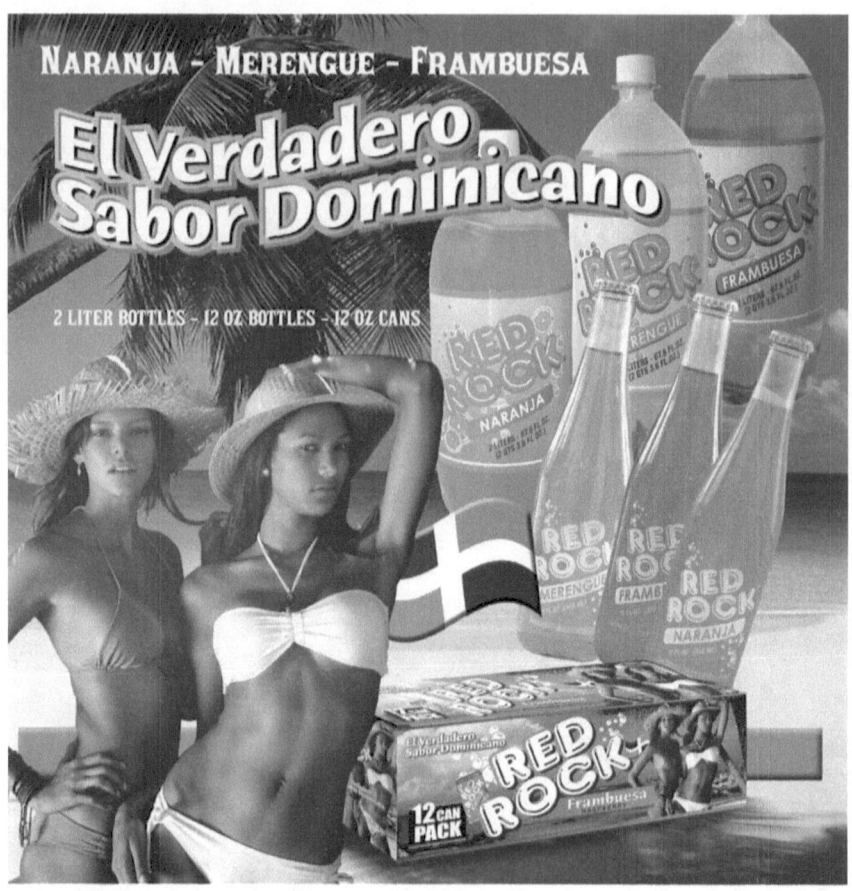

The attention getter here is obvious. The target audience was Dominicans in the NYC metro area hence the Spanish language headlines, Dominican flag and the Caribbean island motif. It also told consumers the various package sizes and formats all of which used the Red Rock logo, as it was familiar to Dominicans as they remembered it back home in the Dominican Republic.

As a side bar: This was assembled mostly in Photoshop and as I was working on it, my late wife walked through my office, glanced at the computer monitor, and asked: "are you getting paid for this?" as she saw the photo of the beautiful girls. I replied, "Yes, and very well."

Since I spent decades working in the soft drink industry as mentioned it will come as no surprise that the number of shelf talkers, danglers and static clings I have designed is countless. For the benefit of any readers interested or skeptical about this industry, I have included an article I wrote a few years back entitled: "*The soft drink industry exposed.*" towards the end of this book.

Shelf talkers are the small heavy paper stock pieces that literally are attached to a store shelf directly below the product. They fold over and are adhered to the shelf and are usually no larger than four inches high and nine inches wide, because that is normally the largest venue stores will allow so that they will not obscure products on the shelf below. Many times the client will insist that the entire product line be shown in hopes that a customer will see a flavor or size not currently in stock and ask the retailer to start carrying that flavor. *This is a big mistake!* Why? Because that rarely, if ever happens and the space taken by a photograph of the entire line is will be hard to see, have small impact and leaves little room in an already small format to call attention to the benefits or other selling points of the product.

The limited space is best used to highlight the product, its unique aspects, image, benefits and/or value price points. Most shelf talkers include either a place for the retailer to write in the price or in some cases when the manufacturer wants the product to be pre-priced (fixed) so the retailer cannot affect the selling price and adversely affect sales.

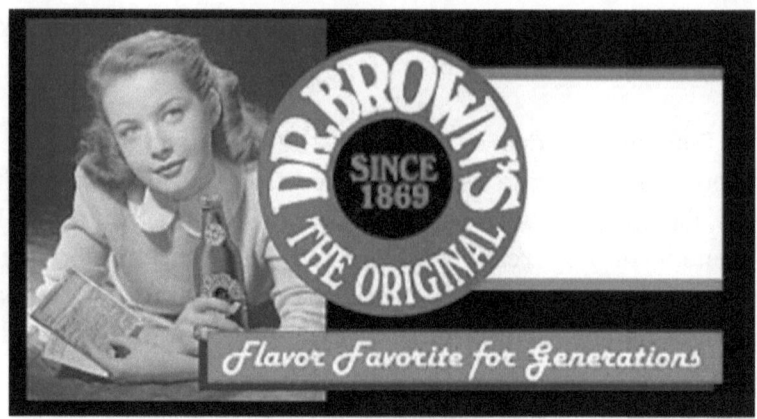

Dr. Brown's soft drinks, a client of mine for over 20 years has a strong following in certain market segments and has been in existence since 1869 *(before my Grandmother was born)* so using a retouched vintage black and white stock photo with a full color bottle in her hands highlights the claim "Flavor Favorite for Generations."

Static Clings are typically used on cold or frozen item cooler doors *(also known as cold boxes)*, are clear or opaque vinyl and as you may suspect they cling to the glass by virtue of static electricity. They are also usually small - typically 4" x 6" or thereabouts so as not to block the view of products inside the box. Hence, from a design viewpoint they are the same as shelf talkers.

Channel strips have similar placement but as the name indicates, these fit in the channels on the edges of store shelves are only about an inch high so the design is often used only for the product logo and possibly a price point.

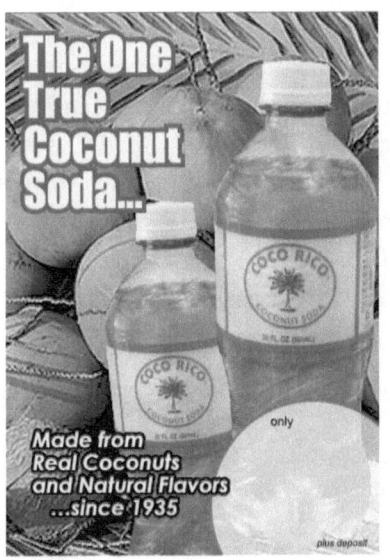
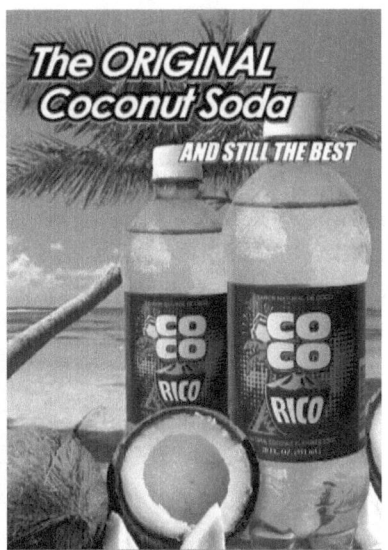

Coco Rico coconut soda was the first and original brand from Puerto Rico. It is a perennial favorite in certain ethnic markets that include not only immigrants from PR but also from Viet Nam who like to use it for cooking. Since then it has faced a lot of competition from imitation products. Hence, the headline and tag line, which say it, is the original and still the best.

As a side bar, one time after I completed a photo shoot in Phoenix, AZ I had a lot of product to dispose of. When a DHL delivery driver of obvious New York City ethic background stopped by to drop off a package, I asked him if he would like some free samples of coconut soda. "Coco Rico brand?" he inquired enthusiastically. "You bet!" I replied, and he took it all. It is not available in Arizona, but he knew the brand name! My client was delighted to hear this.

Banners, sometimes six feet long or longer and sometimes up to six feet high, rarely appear in stores but are very useful for special displays, trade shows, sampling stations or vendor booths indoors or outdoors. Full color banners are getting more affordable but cheaper vinyl cut signs are still in wide use. The graphics on the vinyl cut banners need to be simpler and typically only type or logos in one color and line only (i.e. vector) format. Full color options offer more bang for the buck and are easier to design.

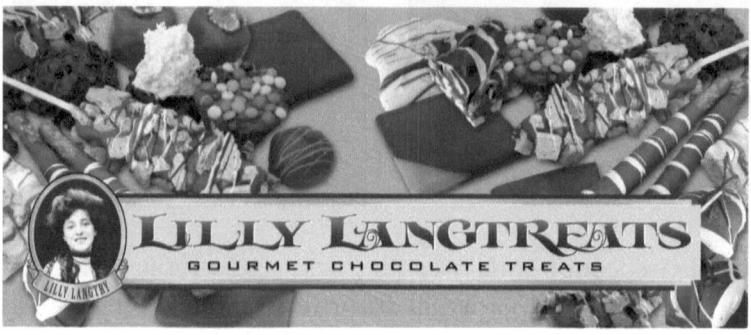

This banner for San Francisco Chocolate Factory showed in full color their most popular products and also promoted the name of their western themed store, so named after the famous western heroine Lily Langtree, at a popular tourist destination named "Rawhide" in Phoenix, Arizona.

Table tents, also as the name implies, sit on tables in stores and frequently in restaurants. They can be cardboard weight fold ups or sometimes, in acrylic holders. In restaurants often, they advertise specials such as "Happy Hour Specials" or specific products or services such as selling sauces or other branded items for customers to consider.

Trade show displays have been included in the point of purchase section because often they use some or all of the above venues. This trade show booth I designed for C&C soft drinks included the background banner, which highlighted their flagship product (C&C Cola) along with their website and Facebook addresses.

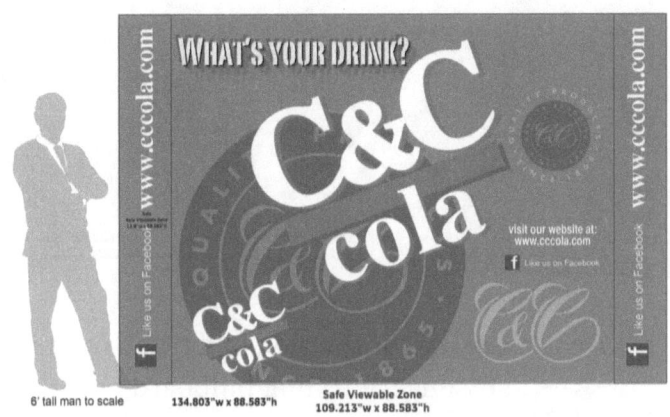

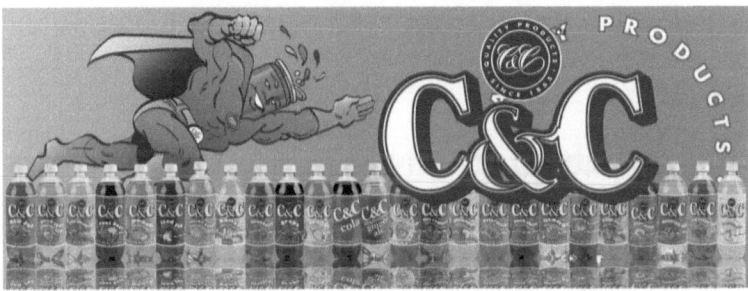

Header on their Facebook page. (also see illustration chapter)

The layout presented to the client showed a silhouette person for scale. There was also a 5-foot cutout of "Cola Man," a character I devised and illustrated. Since the company sells in the metro New York area, I convinced them that a super hero "spokesman" might work well because many comic book creations originated and are set in NYC. He is a regular on their Facebook page and website: www.cccola.com

MISCELLANEOUS

Anything that supports a product or service should tie into the general theme and look of ads, packaging and any other sales literature.

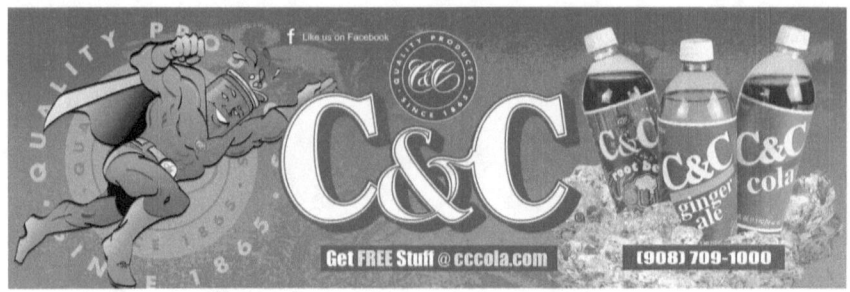

Above is a design for the side of a truck trailer
– in essence, a rolling billboard.

Below is a poster to promote compliance literature.

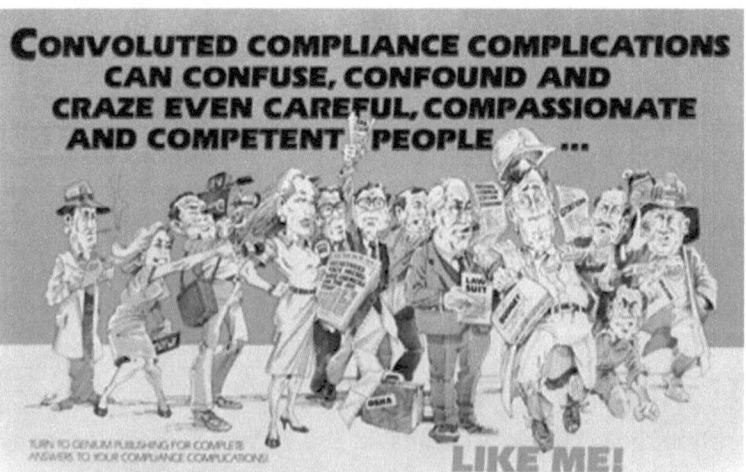

Package Design

This chapter specifically and more accurately is about packaging *graphics* rather than the physical design of package structure as practiced by industrial designers. Although I have been sometimes involved in that to a minor degree as a consultant, I am not a structural engineer! It also focuses on *consumer products, especially food and beverage products* because they fall in the area of my greatest experience and expertise even though over the course of my career, I have designed packages for such diverse things as industrial stone samples aimed at architects and builders, assorted hardware, software, dog treats and once even for chicken manure.

This has been a specialty of mine and my employees since the mid 1980's and one of my clients that I started my business with in 1985 at their prompting, is still a client in 2016. The *design precepts however are the same* as they would be for toilet paper, toys, detergents, bedding, boots, buckles or boat accessories. Except for buying in bulk or buying big like a car or house, almost everything is in a package of some sort: a bag, box, blister pack, can, bottle, wrap, carton or some other type of container.

The purpose of any package is to clearly define the brand name, what is in it, what it does, and why you should buy it. To do this, *and you guessed it*, like any other form of visual communication, *it should follow the 1-2-3 method*. Get attention, communicate clearly and get the viewer to buy it! This is *the ultimate and immediate call to action: take it off the shelf, pay for it and take it home*. All packages are in essence, miniature advertisements most often without the benefit of advertising or collateral help. Doing it successfully is *not* easy.

The overall design, unlike an ad or any collateral must stand out on the shelf right next to a veritable host of your competitor's products. I have never seen a food or beverage product in the personal hygiene, small appliance, or cleaning supplies aisle of a supermarket except when an irresponsible shopper has left it there. All products are grouped by type together in the aisle. Considering that research shows that a consumer needs to notice your product across the aisle and you only have on average 0.7 seconds to capture their interest enough to look closer, it makes this the most difficult aspect of the design. To do this the brand logo and graphics need to be easily read, understood and identified at a glance and from a distance of up to three feet away. This *is not the time* for using trendy, hard to read fonts, cluttered or confusing graphics or something that looks like a crossword puzzle.

The positioning of the product must be clear. Its image, demographic appeal and personality are all part of that positioning. Who is the product aimed at? Is it upscale, fun, a good value, elegant, powerful, dynamic, trend setting, healthy, contemporary, glamorous, or old fashioned? Is it aimed at everyone, men, women, or kids? What is the age demographic: very young, youth, young adults, older adults or all ages? What income brackets: upper, middle or lower income people? What is their ethnicity, White, Hispanic, Black, Asian or other? Before starting, it is imperative to define these questions in all of their various combinations. For example: a wine label for an expensive, upscale product targeting older men should look different than one aimed at young, active women. The former might include silver or gold, black or a dark rich color background, conservative serif fonts and a logo that is emblematic like a coat of arms. The latter may be better with lighter brighter colors, a more youthful upscale and fanciful font and perhaps more "artsy" graphics.

A good example of a client interfering with this research is as follows: An employee at my small design firm named Richard Ingle, was assigned to work on a design for a soft drink product line that was primarily sold to young people in inner city Philadelphia. He did a good job and presented at least three very good options using fonts, colors and graphics that would appeal to this demographic. The owner of the company however, a very wealthy man of advanced years dictated that we use the 1950ish script and oval logo the product had previously and also have pinstripes on the lower half of the label. The result was a label that looked like it belonged on an old-fashioned beer bottle because that was what appealed to him - but not his customers. The product is still being produced in small quantities only because he has personal affection for his brand. The sales figures are dismal at best instead of having the opportunity for the upsurge that well redesigned packages often create.

There are way too many graphic, typographic and substrate options to enumerate here in less than 1,000 pages. Some of the practical considerations are at the end of this chapter. When in doubt, do your homework, go to stores, websites and other sources to find out what may appeal to the varying demographics your client or boss has defined. If they or you have not done this research - *don't start to work!* Your boss or client may grumble, but in the long run, they will respect your professionalism.

Benefits before features!

Clearly extoll the benefits of the product in easily understood ways. Is it low calorie, sugar free, gluten free, sodium free, have no MSG, organic, non GMO, caffeine free, easy to prepare or use, healthy, or energizing? These are not afterthoughts to find some room for, they are selling points that help a consumer decide to buy. Don't assume that because you know what an ingredient does that the buyer does. "Contains B vitamins, taurine and ginseng extract" means nothing unless you also say that these are energy enhancing ingredients. *(In energy drinks, they do however conveniently leave out the fact that the caffeine content adds most of the zip!)* "Vitamin enhanced" means little unless you say what specific vitamins. And if an ingredient is new to the public or has a technical name, you had better explain why "XyZingo" is good.

For example: Long before Stevia became a commonly known organic natural sweetener, I went to great lengths on the front and side panels for a new product called "Z" cola and orange, to explain where it came from and why it was a healthy alternative to cane sugar, aspartame, acesulfame potassium or high fructose corn syrup. The company was eventually sold and the product is now called Zevia.

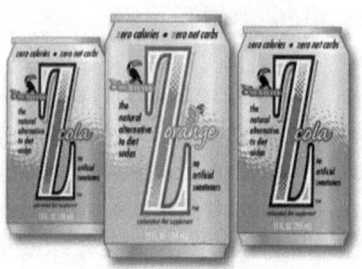

Consumer norms: Early in my career, I learned the hard way not to ignore consumer-recognized norms. I once designed a label for cola that was dark brown because that is the color of the liquid product. I was ignorant of colors and graphics that consumers have come to understand often without even reading the label. Brown is for Root Beer! Colas are expected to be either red or red white and blue. Why? Because the brand leaders, Coke and Pepsi are those colors! You could almost put the brand and product identity in any language or just made up jargon but if it is in a 2-liter plastic bottle with a dark brown, nearly black liquid inside almost all people will think it is a cola. Another example is coffee. If the can is red, chances are it is regular. If it is green, it is decaffeinated. Many products have these norms. Find out what they are before starting any project or you will be laughed at like I was.

As an item of humor, not long ago Coca Cola introduced a reformulated version of its flagship brand yet again. Apparently, some marketing or brand manager genius, who apparently never consulted a soft drink package design expert, approved a white can for this introduction. With soda, white, silver or sometimes light pastel colors are the consumer norm for DIET drinks. I would have told them for free just to add Coke to my client list! When sales tanked the package was revised. *As a side bar:* soft drink bottlers take great care in labeling for fear (mortal terror is more like it) of putting a regular sweetened drink into a diet package. They don't want to risk the moral or legal risk of putting a diabetic into insulin shock, the hospital or the grave.

Equally important are consumer expected norms such as value/price points, special offers or premiums. RED on YELLOW, often in an ugly snipe, bellyband or starburst is the norm. Get over it and use it. "GET 20% MORE" - "SALE PRICE" - "NEW" - "IMPROVED" - "FREE OFFER" are all very important for SELLING more product. Making them blend in with esthetically appealing colors is a bad plan. Don't do it.

Major brands, Off brands and Store brands.

Consumer products generally fall into these three categories. I have rarely in my career worked on major brands, the mega conglomerate corporations with national or international sales. Jolly Rancher brand soft drinks licensed by Hershey Foods (which owns the brand) and manufactured and distributed by Elizabeth Beverages is the only notable exception. While it was nice to have them on my client list and drop their name at social gatherings, I found the experience to be eventually constricting because of corporate standard graphic guidelines. And frustrating, because the marketing people who know a whole lot about candy know very little about soft drinks and eventually their graphic dictates killed sales of the soft drinks.

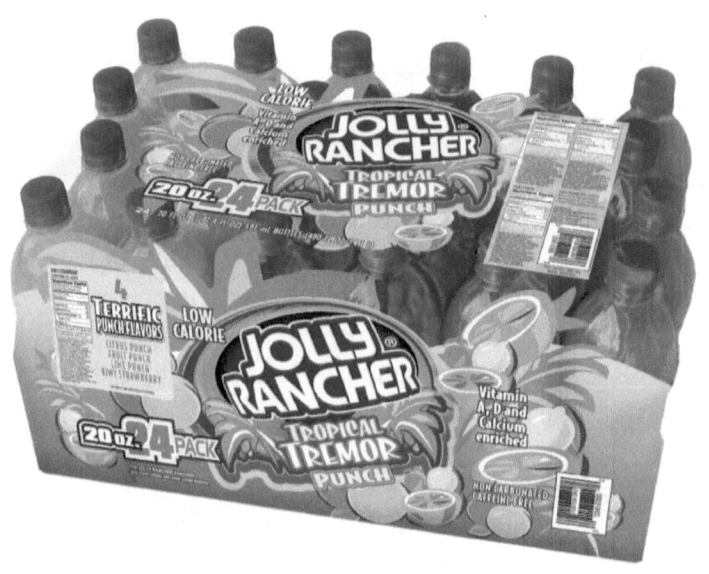

Cott, a major corporation, which does private label brands internationally, was equally frustrating because of their unwieldy corporate structure replete with managers, brand groups and committees, which leads to delays, confusion, meaningless dictates and the like. I was once reprimanded for failure to put the mandatory 10 state deposit information on a label. *I had to gently inform them that it was a non-carbonated drink that required only Maine and California return information at the time.*

Often the graphics managers proclaimed the designs not suitable for the print process *until my client and I pointed out that the same label had been printed for years without problems* before they ever got involved.

Cott Canada, promised me a LOT of new business if I conformed to their computer and software platform. Needing the income at the time, I shelled out for the additional hardware and software. *The amount of work that was sent to me: ZERO.*

Cott Mexico was easier to deal with and I did a lot of work for them despite the language barrier and regulatory requirements, but when the group manager left, his replacement never contacted me no doubt to give the business to a friend or crony.

That having been said, or rather griped about, I do not miss or regret not walking with the big guys. I made a good living without them thank you.

Off brands:

Off brands is a catch all term for *regional, local or boutique specialty products.* This area is often unknown or belittled without good reason. These types of brands account for a large percentage of products sold in America and elsewhere. One of these days, I might research the exact number but from my anecdotal evidence based on experience, I know this to be true, especially when combined with the next section entitled store brands.

These brands have all the design challenges of major brands but almost totally without the support of name recognition and huge advertising budgets. The package HAS to do all the work sometimes aided by some point of purchase material, which is difficult for them to manage for lack of money and human resources to get it into the stores.

This category along with the following is where I made much of my money and reputation. Instead of corporate hierarchies, more often than not I worked directly with the owner(s), CEOs, General Managers or sales managers. Decisions are decisive and quick if sometimes biased. You know who you are dealing with and can approach the projects with individuals in mind instead of nameless committees.

One client whom I worked with for many years had a quirk that I quickly learned to adapt to. He often would describe or worse yet give me a "kitchen table" type sketch of what he wanted. If I skipped showing him what he asked for which was invariably amateurish, unworkable and ugly and just showed him a better solution, he grew petulant because he did not see what he asked for and summarily dismissed my designs. If, however I showed him exactly what he *thought* he wanted and waited for him to see how bad it was and *then* showed him alternates that were infinitely better, he responded with enthusiasm. It made for a better relationship and better design.

There have been times that I have enjoyed being part of this category and seeing it kick butt on major brands at times. Once after work I was in the local supermarket shopping for supper and I got to watching an older couple shopping. The woman had quite a few bottles of national brand soft drinks in their cart. She paused by an end aisle display of British American brand soda (which I designed for the aforementioned client) to look at something else. I was not close enough to hear the words exchanged, but as she turned back to the cart, the man pointed at the British American. It looked good and was way less expensive than the National Brands because of its distribution method.* They removed the national brands from their cart and replaced them with British American, leaving the national brands in their place on the display. I wished I had a video camera with me. It would have made a dandy commercial!

* There are two ways products get onto store shelves. Direct store delivery (DSD) and Warehouse Delivery. With DSD, the manufacturer maintains a fleet of delivery trucks and drivers that bring their products to each individual store and sees to their placement in their allotted space on the shelves, also the placement of point of sale materials. This costs money. Some manufacturers deliver their products directly to the store chain's warehouse. It is then delivered to individual stores along with all sorts of other products and placed on the shelves by store employees. This usually, but not always, allows for a lower price point but also leaves little opportunity for in-store POP, and the organization on the shelf is sometimes poor.

Boutique or specialty products are more difficult because the budget is usually very limited which from a practical viewpoint restricts the amount of time you can invest in the work unless it is for Uncle Joe, your brother-in-law Tom or a good friend which is often a lose-lose situation. Sometimes some extra expenditure of time can be worth it for the recognition or because sometimes these "little clients" evolve into bigger companies. They remember often who helped them grow. And sometimes it can be just plain fun to work on a shoestring budget.

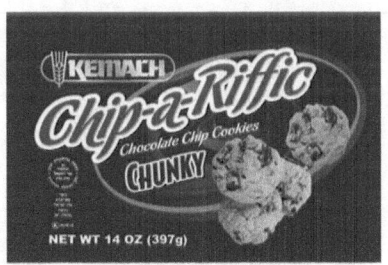

The above was actually designed for the client via a printer I had a long relationship with. It was a specialty product aimed at Jewish kosher consumers. Because of the niche, market it was in it never grew into a bigger brand.

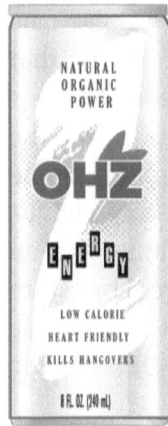 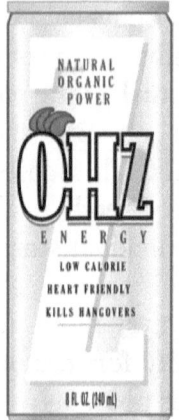 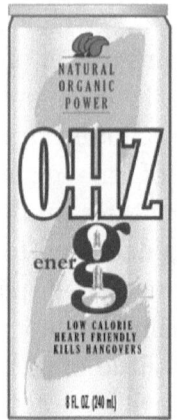 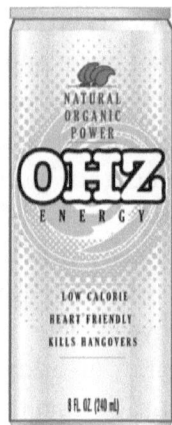

This product is currently under preliminary development as I write this. I do not expect it to go far but I have a long-term relationship with the client and am willing to humor him and I'm also being paid!

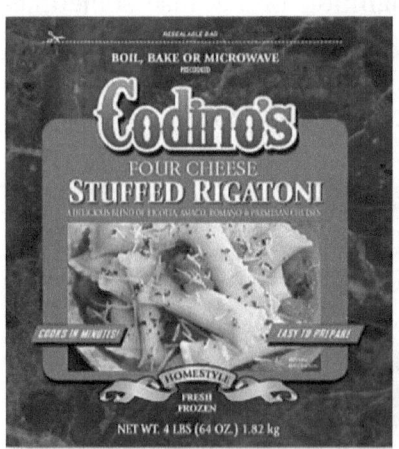 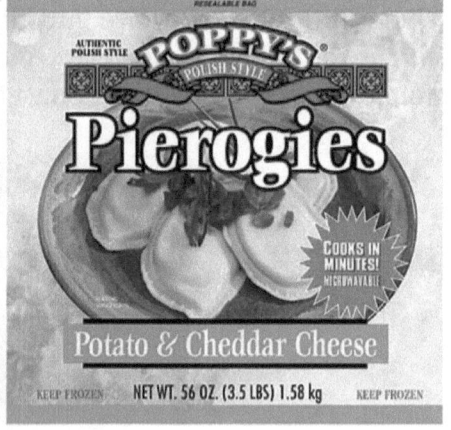

Codino's is a major regional pasta manufacturer who primary sells in bulk to the food service industry, but they had some success with consumer store brands

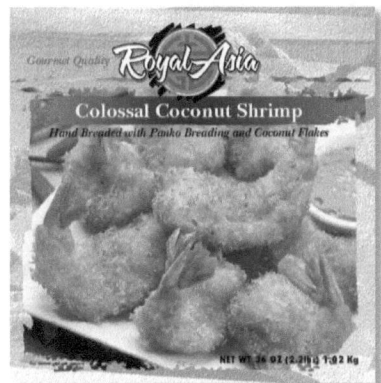 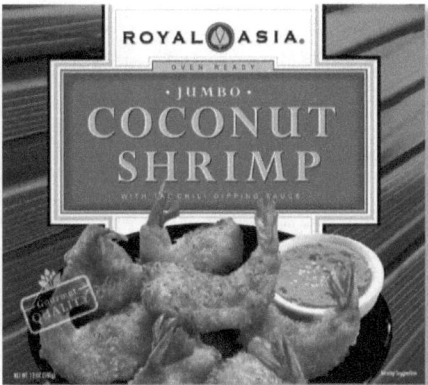

These designs illustrate two divergent and in my opinion poor branding decisions on the part of the client. The one on the left, I designed to upgrade their existing line of frozen Asian specialties. It features a dominant brand logo with a subordinate product identity and a BIG prepared product photo.

The one on the right was dictated by their new brand manager who used to work in the private label store brand business. It has a small brand logo and huge product I.D. It looks like a store brand! If you swapped out Royal Asia with Kroger, Safeway, Acme or any other supermarket logo that is what it would resemble. It isn't horrible design – just poor branding.

Clients often see the designer as the low man (or woman) on the totem pole. No matter how many years of experience you may have, you are ultimately "just a pair of hands" in their minds. "I am paying the bill, so I want what I want," is a common refrain.

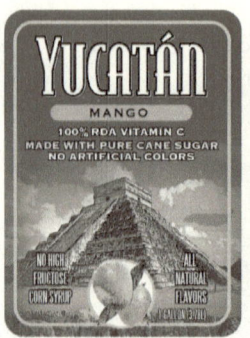
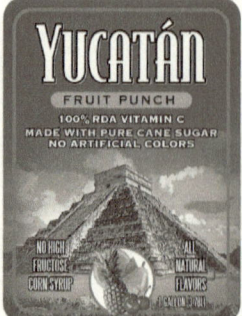
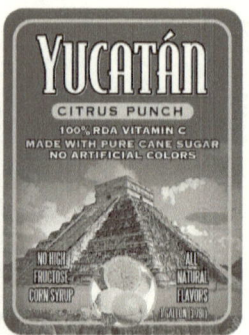

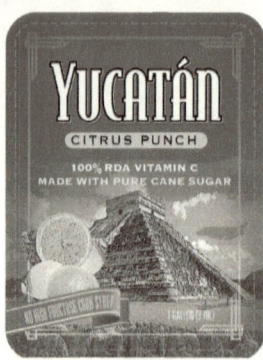
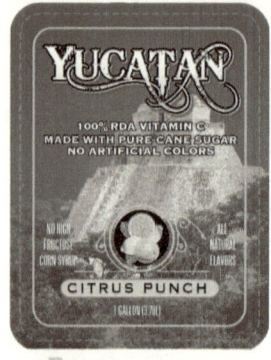

A   B

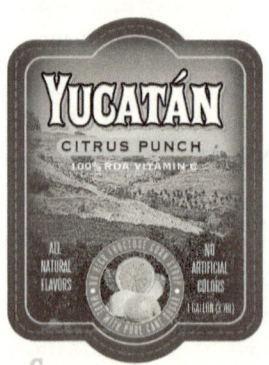
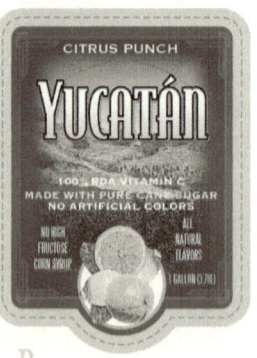

C   D

Four design variants presented to the client and on top the final rendition in the three flavors. The client requested something that resembled an old-fashioned wood produce crate label even though it would appear on a plastic bottle.

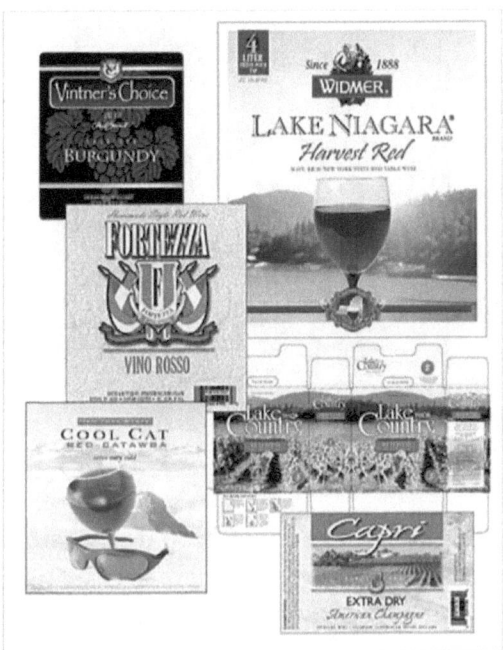

A sampling of wine labels and cartons designed for Batavia Wine Cellars.

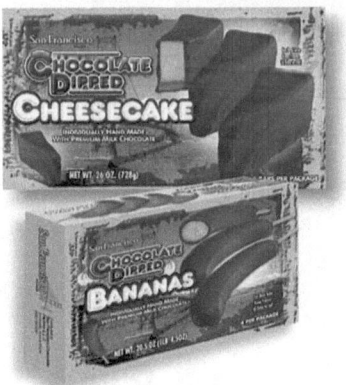

In the above, I broke my own branding rules because in this case the company, San Francisco Chocolate Factory was little known so I made "Chocolate Dipped" appear as though it was the brand.

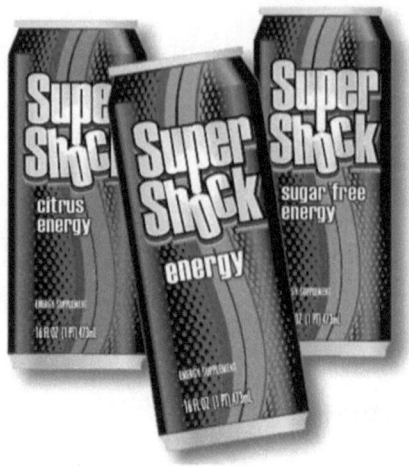

A line of energy drinks designed for Monarch Custom Beverages in Atlanta, Georgia. These were the original offering but have now expanded to several more flavor options. It is still on the market.

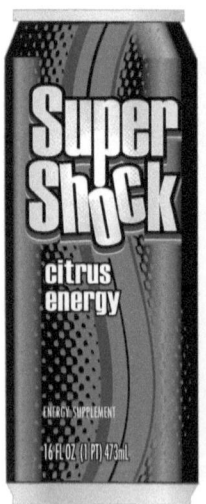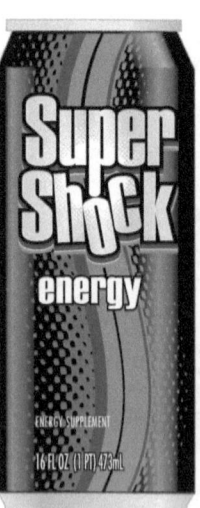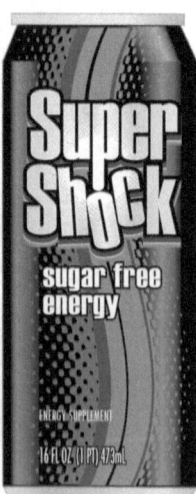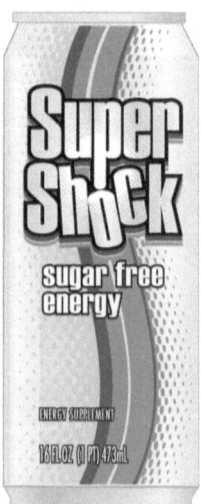

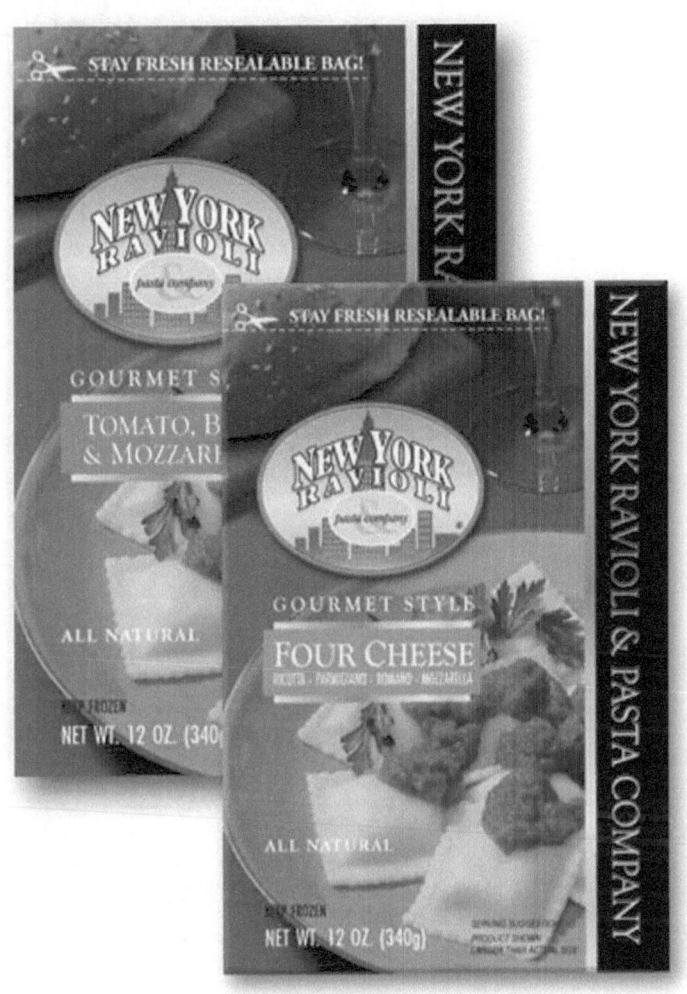

These frozen pasta bags for New York Ravioli were for their new premium line of products. The rich colors and black side stripe with gold type project a premium image. In this case, the product tasted VERY good so the premium look and price was justified!

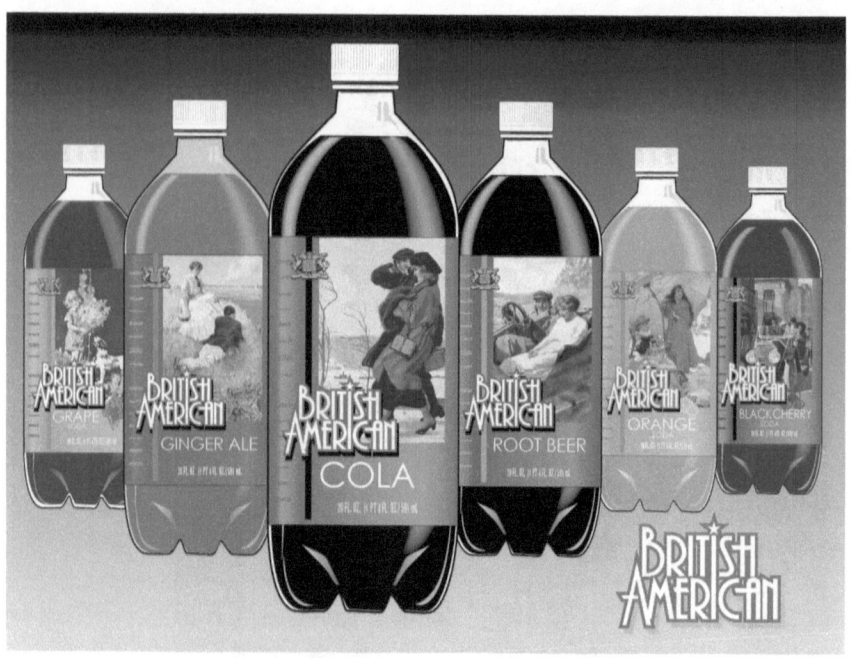

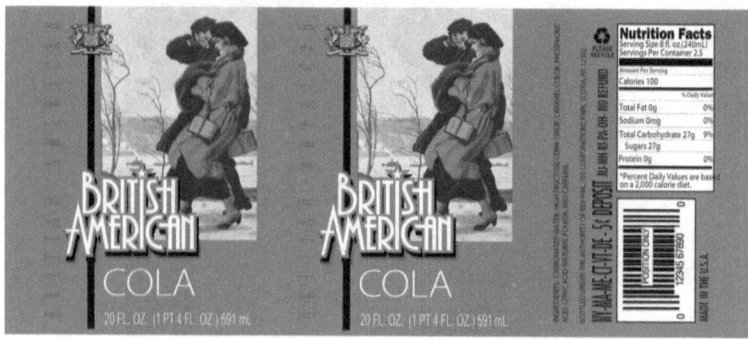

This was and is one of my favorite labels for and old brand badly needing some new life. The vintage illustrations reflected the colors of the flavors and looked like they just stepped out of history. Unfortunately, the brand was dropped because it was too expensive to support in the marketplace in addition to the clients other brands. Slotting fees, that is the "rent" manufacturers pay to be on a super market shelf often are in the range of $10,000 per product whether it sells or not.

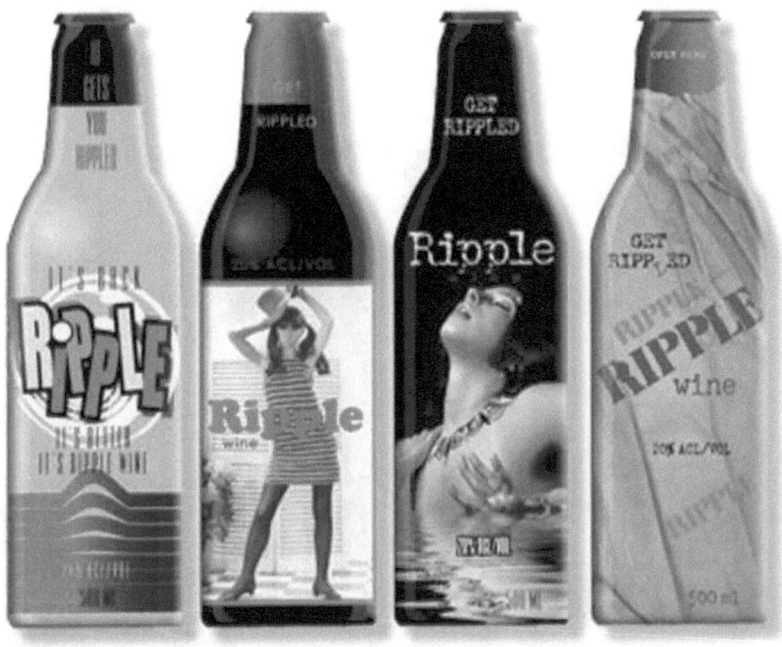

Sometimes your best work just goes into the archives because the product was soon cancelled. Above are some damn good options for a client proposed revival of an old and popular brand to be packaged in an aluminum bottle. The concept however, was flawed from the very beginning. Ripple was a strong low-end product – cheap wine college students drank and made famous by the TV character Fred Sanford (Sanford & Son) back in the 1970s. (Champipple). Today's college kids would never go for this and the nostalgia lost on them.

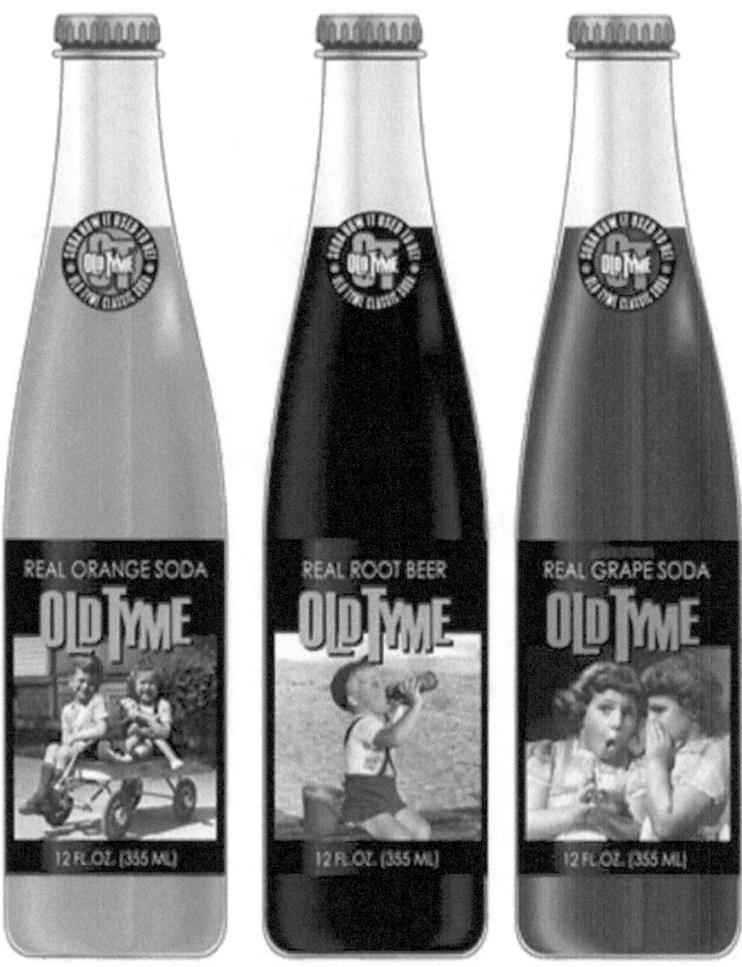

Sometimes the client just can't get past the old design to move on. The below design proposed black and white old time photos juxtaposed to color logos and other type to help connote the individual flavor, similar in approach to the very successful Jones Soda brand.

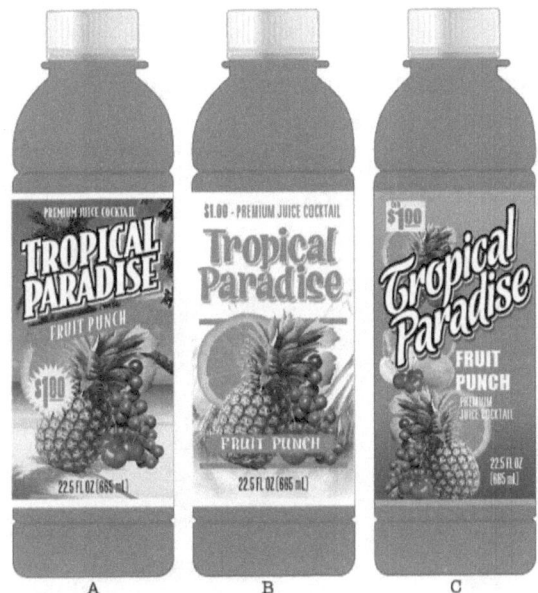

Three design variants.

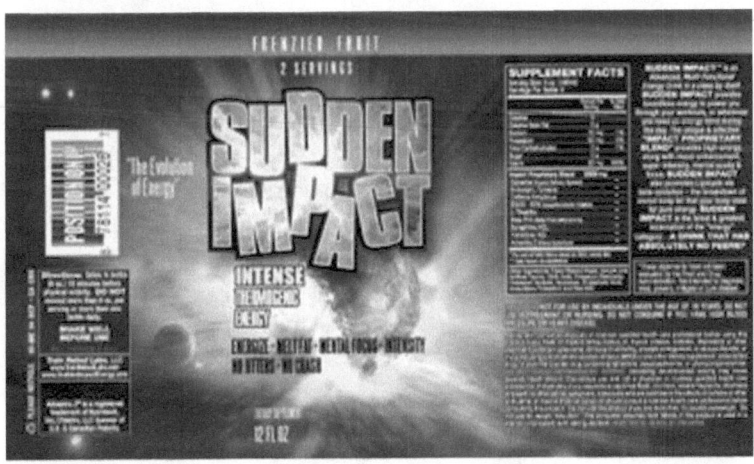

Some other samples of design. With Sudden Impact, you can see how much real estate is gobbled up with mandatory information.

Some other varied projects of note:

- Dr. Browns 12 oz. glass upgraded from the old design
- Clear 'N' Natural for Adirondack Beverages
- Wadda Juice – juice & water aimed at mothers of toddlers
- Cuba Libra 6 pack wrap for Cott, Mexico –
  note the placement of 6 pack!

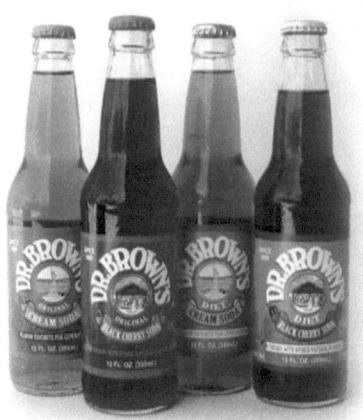
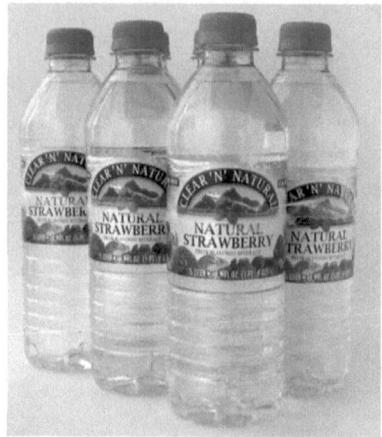
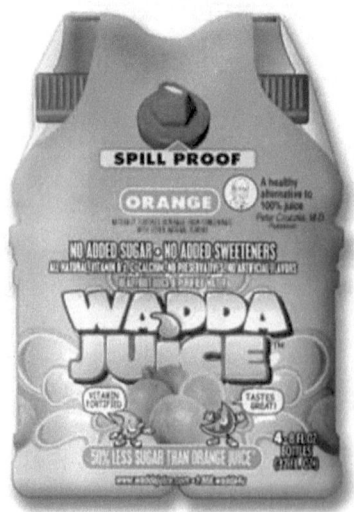
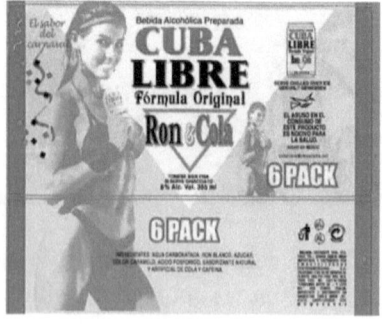

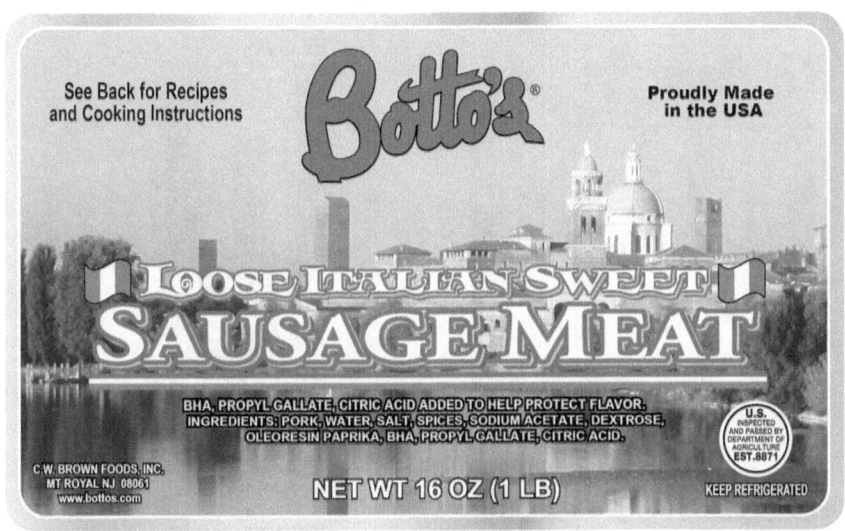

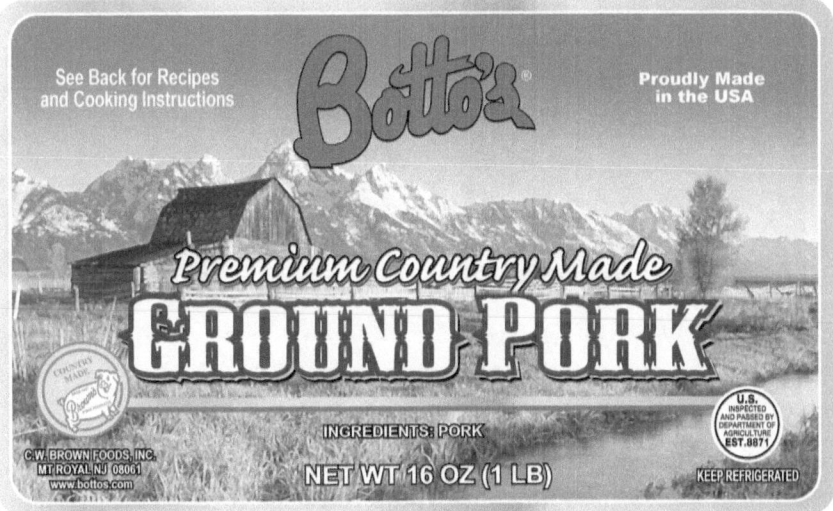

Fresh ground meat labels for Botto's – Note the selling and mandatory seals and statements. The constant in the label is the logo and general layout. Typography and photos carry feel of the products. Since the product itself was in a clear tray there is no need to show it on the label.

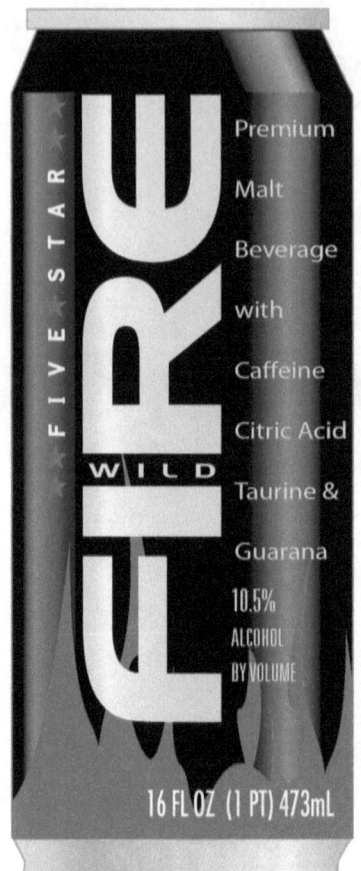 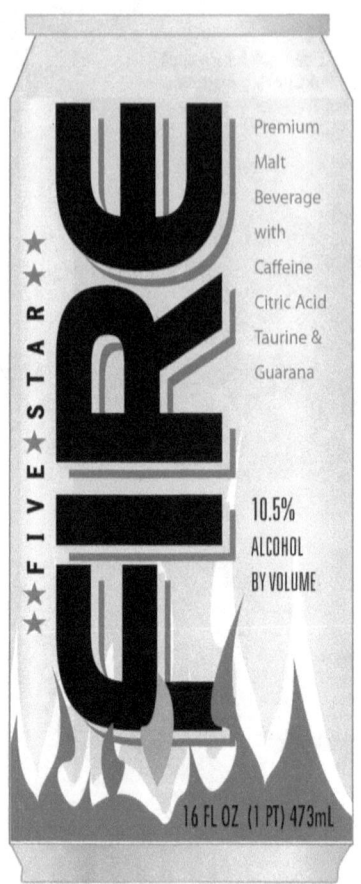

Above are preliminary designs for a new and very strong malt beverage. The alcohol by volume statement has strict regulations regarding size, which have been adhered to. Wine is typically 9-11% - this stuff is strong!

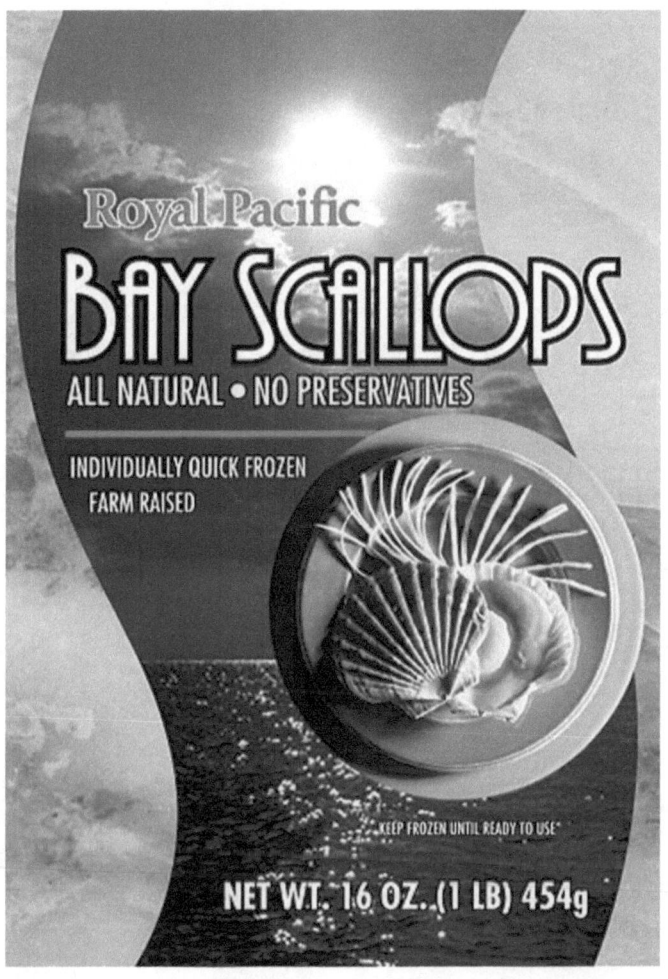

While it's good to have longer term relationships, designers always have "one night stands." The clients you do only one or two projects for and not much more for a variety of reasons. But some of them are gems in the miscellaneous category in your portfolio. This one timer was a low budget affair too. All the images were stock or from the archives.

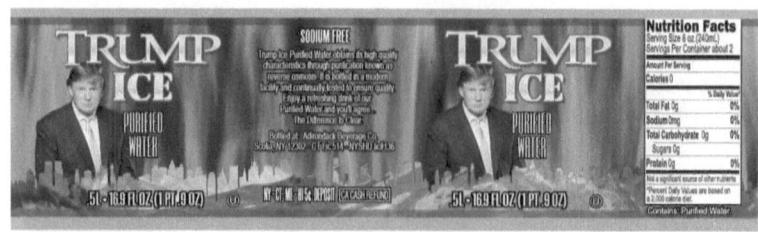

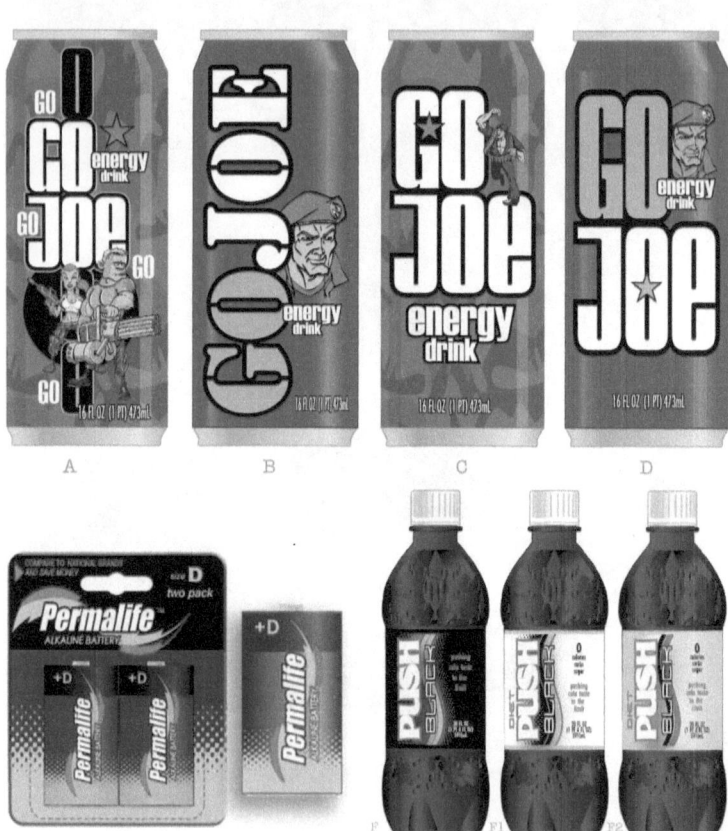

Some of my more unusual assignments: 1. Donald Trump before he became a presidential candidate. On one version of this I had to retouch his hair! 2. An energy drink based on G.I Joe for Monarch Custom Beverages. 3. Permalife batteries for Hengwei in China. 4. After the client had an intern do a design for this and it *failed miserably*, I was hired to do it right.

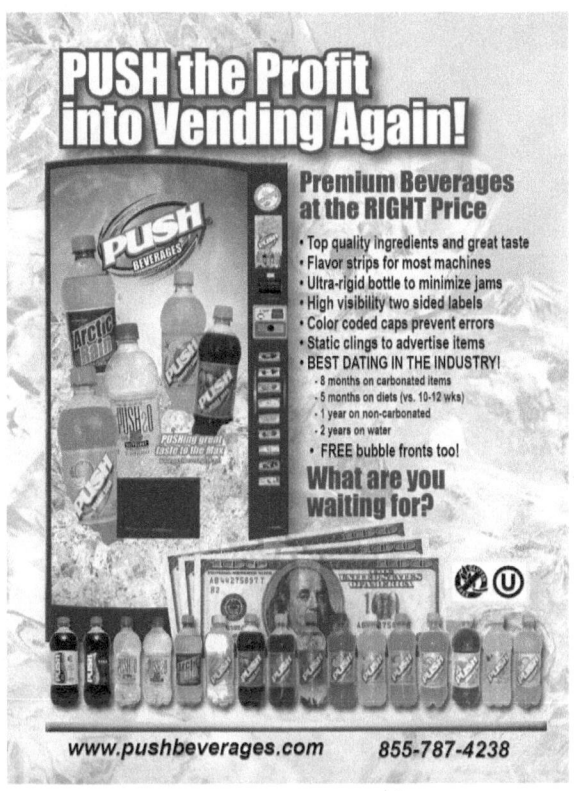

I designed all the packaging and the vending machine fronts, which in itself was an exercise in pulling teeth*, but this is one of *countless variations* for a trade ad promoting their vending program. For vending machine fronts clients typically want to just play it safe ... *put the product in ice like everyone else.*

NOTE: I resigned this account because of the micromanagement on the part of the client.

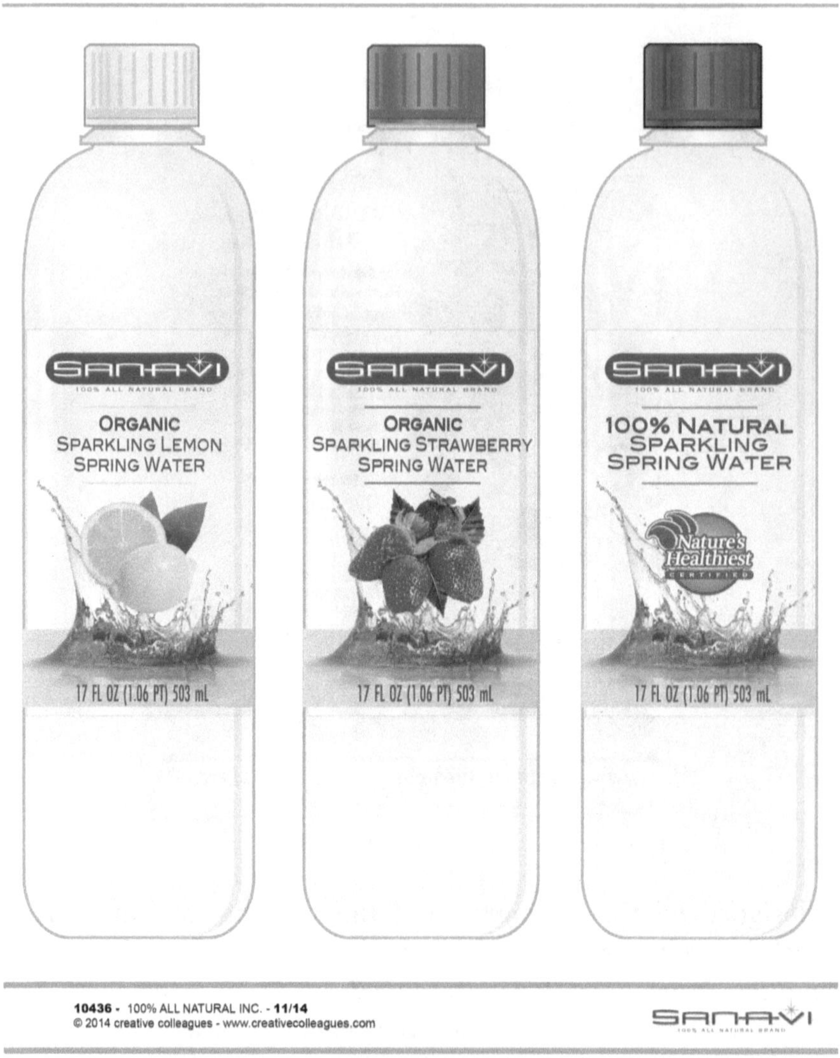

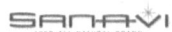

Above is a proposed design that competed with another designer's submission. I came in second place – BUT was paid. Unpaid contest are unfair, a waste of time and unethical.

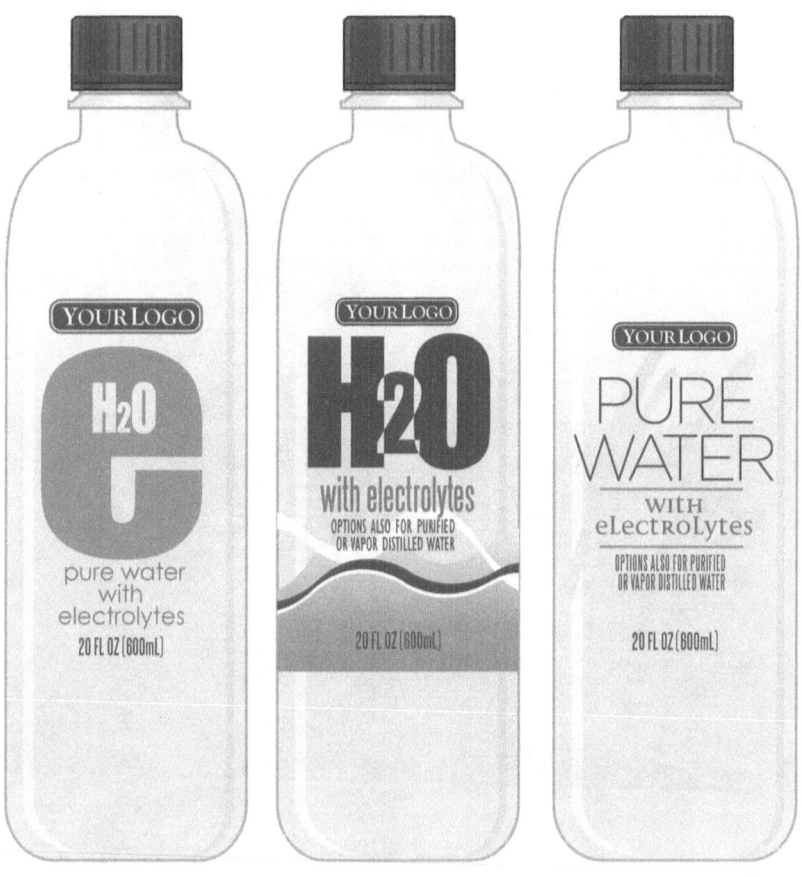

Above shows variants in design approaches.
These were for a company proposal to secure private label
business for their bottling facility.

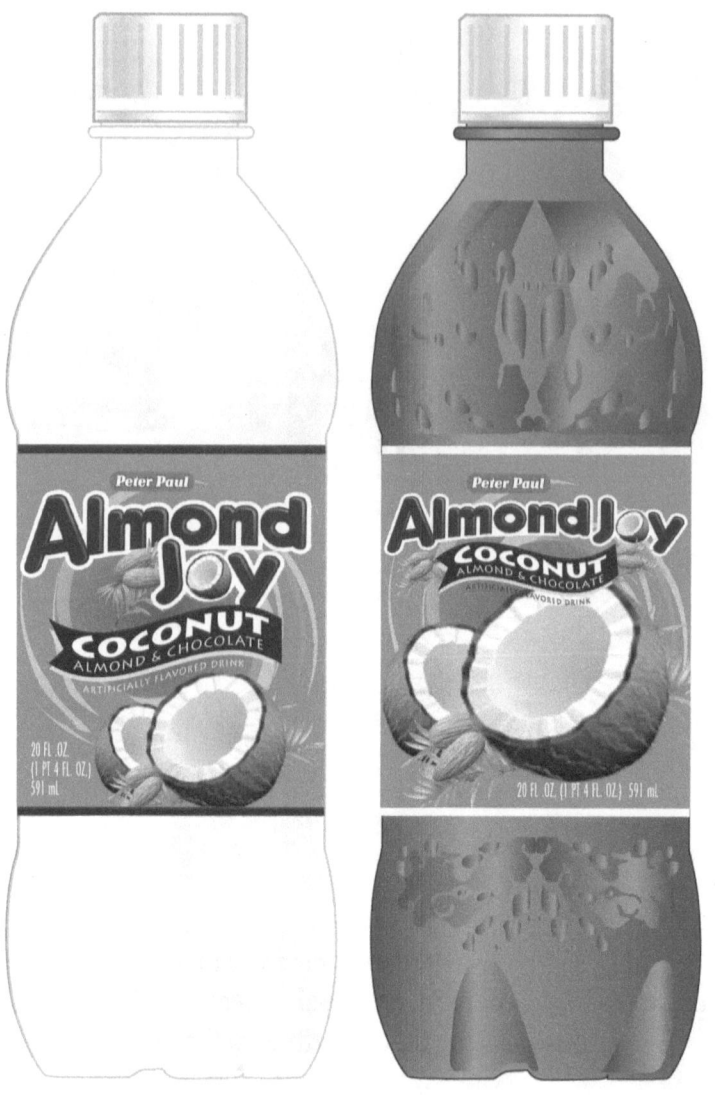

Above are variables for a project as we were narrowing down the concept – Not only the label but optional product color.

Store Brands:

Store brands, also known as private label brands, now make up a huge segment of the marketplace. These products that carry their store brand logo from soft drinks, paper towels, frozen fish, canned green beans to trash bags etc. are all made by major manufacturers and are sometime qualitatively equal to or in some cases superior to the major brands. All of my soft drink accounts did private label packing and most of my food accounts did also in addition to their own brands. Once rather haphazard in design they now have corporate marketing departments and well defined but usually flexible graphic standards especially on how logos, quality assurance seals and the like, need to be treated for uniformity across product lines. Within these boundaries, there is usually plenty of room for good creative design.

Perceived value is a topic I saved for this section although it applies to all the others too. When store brands first came onto the scene, their package design was usually very poor. It screamed CHEAP even if the quality of what was inside the package was pretty good. The upside of this was that shoppers on a tight budget many times would instinctively just grab the store brand assuming it cost less even if a major or regional brand was in reality intrinsically less expensive or was on special. Since then stores have continually upgraded the design of their products to compete with branded products. Some store products even have premium grade offerings now. I have often thought that stores should consider offering another version of their private label products to take advantage of the lower perceived value image for their strictly budget minded shoppers. Call it the "value line" and make it look cheap!

For all types and modes of products, it is best for us to keep "perceived value" in mind. If the product you are designing the package for costs a lot of money, it darn well better dress like it. If it is a value product, typically sold at a low price it darn well better not look too expensive. Rules, however, meant to be bent also indicate that sometimes a low cost item that looks like the top of the line may sell well also.

From a strictly business point of view I have enjoyed the design challenges but also profited handsomely from doing private label design and production. Most if not all of the work in this area I have done for the manufacturers whom I have a steady relationship with, not directly for the store chains. They trust a designer who also handles their own brands, knows the rules and makes their job easier. And they know pretty much what they will pay for it since the manufacturer is on the hook for the artwork.

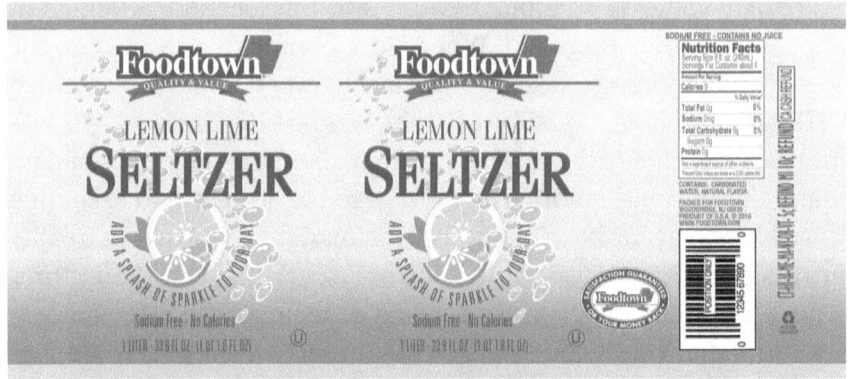

This is the example noted in the introduction. The phrase, "Add a splash of sparkle" had been written twenty years before it finally saw use.

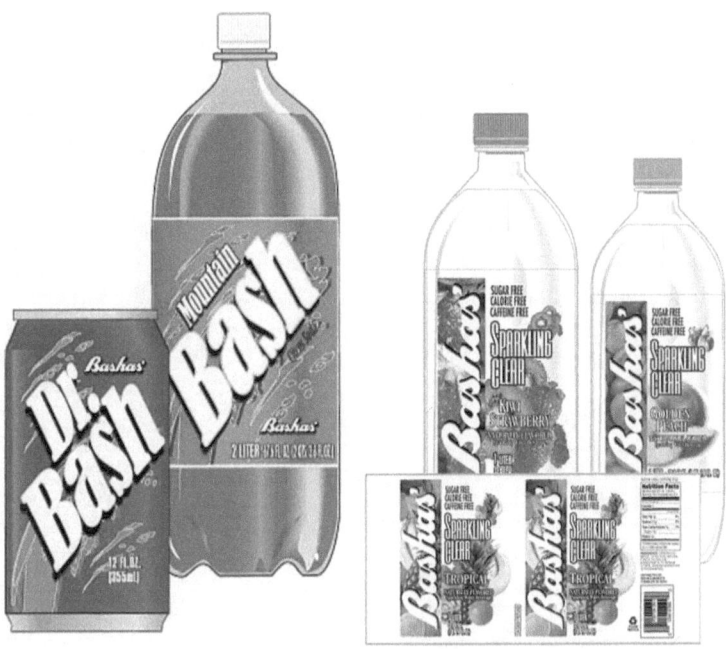

Above are examples of store brands. In the case of Dr. Bash and Mountain Bash for Basha's markets, these were devised to look like name brands.

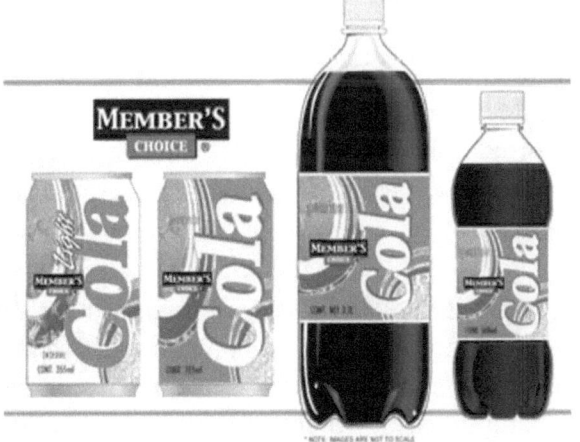

Member's choice - yet another mega store brand

Know the Rules:

In the early days of package design including patent medicines, you could put almost anything on the label, true or untrue, as long as it fit and sold the stuff.

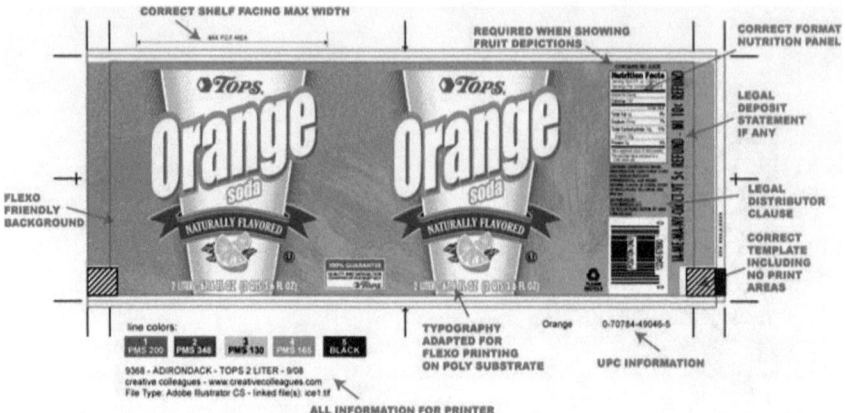

Today, for most packages there are a plethora of regulatory agencies including the FDA, NLEA and BATF among others that have set down rules and guidelines that must be adhered to regarding content, claims, size relationships and other government regulations. *Details are important!* These often change rapidly. While you may not be the one ultimately responsible for compliance, you MUST be aware of the ones that exist in the areas in which you are working. And know when to ask.

After over 35 years in the business, I often know nearly as much as the manufacturers in this regard and always more than the clients. It can be a struggle at times to explain to a client that the mandatory claims must be where they need to be and in the size required.

Space is also taken up by UPC bar codes, nutrition panels, deposit statements, allergen warnings, quality assurance claims and the like. All of these have legal size, placement and color rules. In many cases, label panels are getting smaller for ecological and economic reasons. Before this (and I remember those days) there was much more real estate available to deal with the design elements.

Designers must also be up to speed with various print processes and limitations for certain materials and substrates. What is possible to print on paper is not possible on polypropylene bags, wraps or labels, corrugated boxes or aluminum cans. You will often be required to work hand in hand with the printers.

Your work must also be pragmatic! All packaging must adhere to the limitations of the printing process and the materials used. No design is acceptable that is not printable or challenges the process so much as to be cost prohibitive. Work with manufacturers and printers BEFORE beginning the design process or you will risk wasting time and money! Also getting fired.

Summary

Working in packaging can be rewarding for your ego and your bank account. Walking into a store and seeing your work on the shelf is FUN! Being able to point it out to a companion is even better. When my new in-laws who are Jewish found out I designed Dr. Brown's soda (a Jewish favorite deli brand) they were very impressed. In addition to this, new products are always in the works and require graphic design.

Packages are always in need of revising for regulatory or technical reasons and line extensions (adding more variations like new flavors, types or diet versions) are common.

For example: In 1993, the NLEA nutrition box standards were introduced as regulations by the FDA. Every food package needed to be revised to accommodate this and since new printing plates would also be required, many companies decided to upgrade the design of their products at the same time. This was a BIG boost for business to designers and printers alike. It also led to better design and profits for the manufacturers.

Another example: As different package and label, sizes are introduced often for production efficiency or economy you will be called upon to adjust the graphics to accommodate these new parameters. When a client of mine switched their 20 oz. bottle size to accommodate Pepsi in their plant, every product had to be revised. This may not always be great fun but is paying work that will help you pay the rent, mortgage, car payment and put food on your table!

To quote an old high school teacher of mine: "You have to eat."

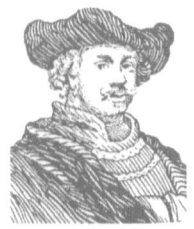

Illustration:

"The reports of my death have been greatly exaggerated."
--- Mark Twain

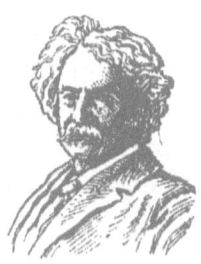

Digital stock illustration has had a major impact on both the illustration and photography world but illustration is hardly a dead end career. In fact, the stock options have opened venues for illustrators to sell their work for a wide variety of uses and to repeat audiences on a royalty basis through many on-line digital sources like fotolia.com and many others. Books, magazines, advertising agencies, and design studios are just the tip of the iceberg for selling illustration.

Developing a distinctive style or styles is still the norm for most of us. I was fortunate in my career to not only sell my work to studios and agencies but also be the art director for much of my own work. I therefore could prostitute myself to me! Pimp, customer and deliverer of services all rolled in one. I say that because like all other forms of commercial visual "art", we create *what the customer or client wants to portray.* If you want to just "do your own thing" become a fine artist and hope people like your work enough to buy it!

Conventional media like graphite, ink, and paint applied by things like pencils, pens and brushes are still being done but digital art is growing geometrically because of its style, complexity and speed of execution (in most cases anyway). No matter what the tool or media however, *the ability to actually be able to draw is an essential skill!* Even art that will eventually be used in an animation or a video game usually starts out as a sketch on paper.

Unless you land a job with a studio, the profession is usually a solitary one. Developing a marketable style, promoting (selling) yourself and pounding the pavement or cruising cyber space and actually getting paid assignments takes time. Lots of time.

The professor I introduced this book with once told me in his office that he aspired one time to get a job at Walt Disney studios. He did and he lasted a week once he realized what an assembly line type of process it was. For years, you might be the "Mickey Mouse red shorts color person" before moving up and on to better and more challenging roles. The places at the top of this chain, like animator, head animator or director are few. It is not all that different today. You may start out as the lighting texturizer for "Bling-Bling" or a background person, just another cog in a BIG wheel of production. If the industry however suits your talents and temperament, far be it from me to discourage you. I will cover some more ground on this topic in the Careers and Business chapters following.

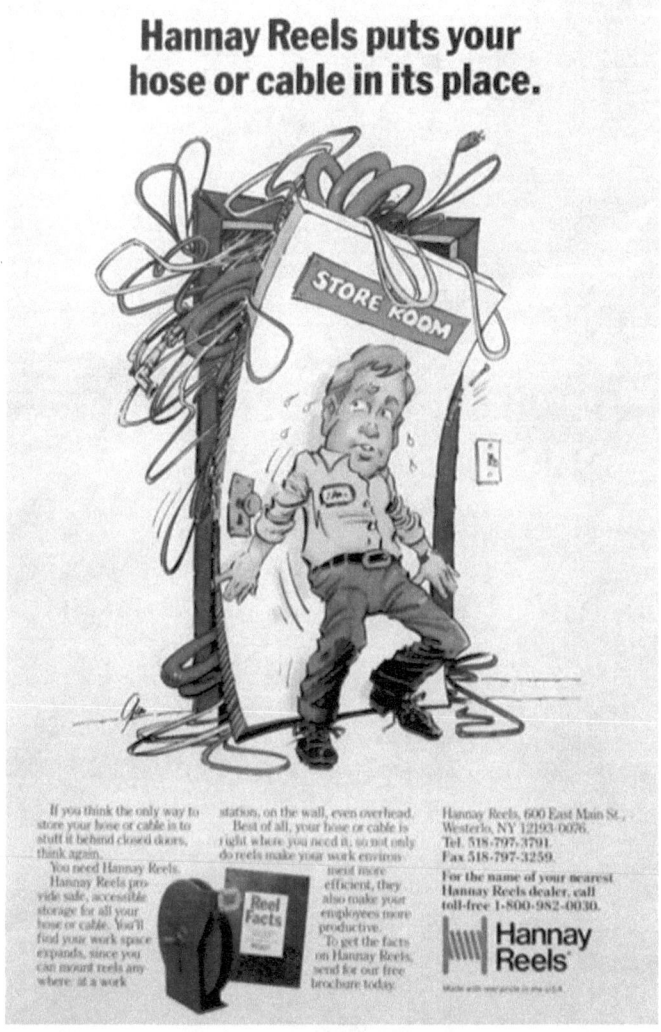

Cartoon or humorous illustration has always been a BIG part of my mix. This was for an agency client, Wolkcas Advertising in NY, Rob DeLuke art director. Ironically, it was the agency that took over the Hannay Reels account that my previous employer had for many years and which I worked on frequently.

Note: I was much influenced in my career by the late Jack Davis of Mad Magazine notoriety or fame depending on how you view it.

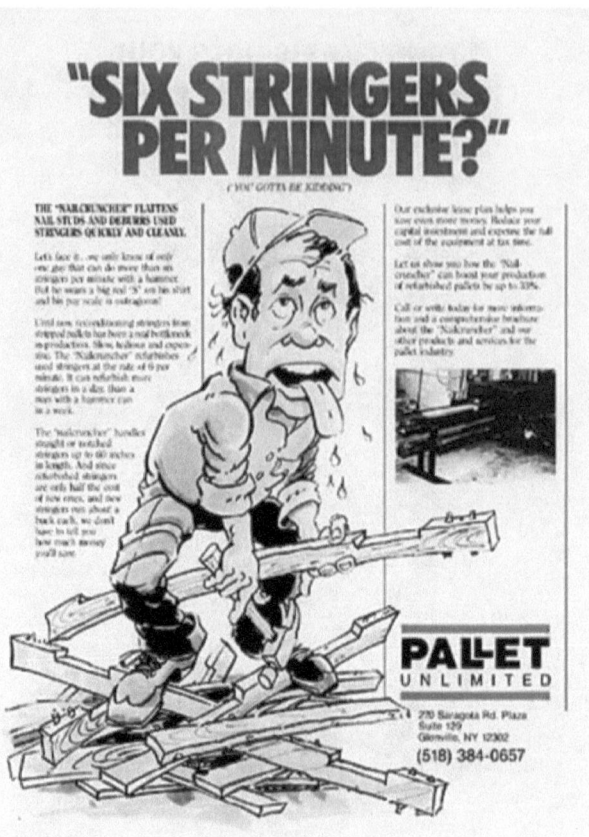

An ad series which I also wrote and designed.
Again, note the Jack Davis influence

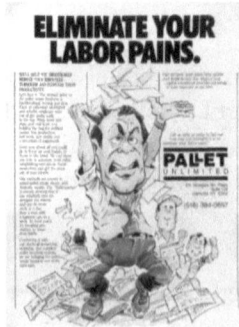

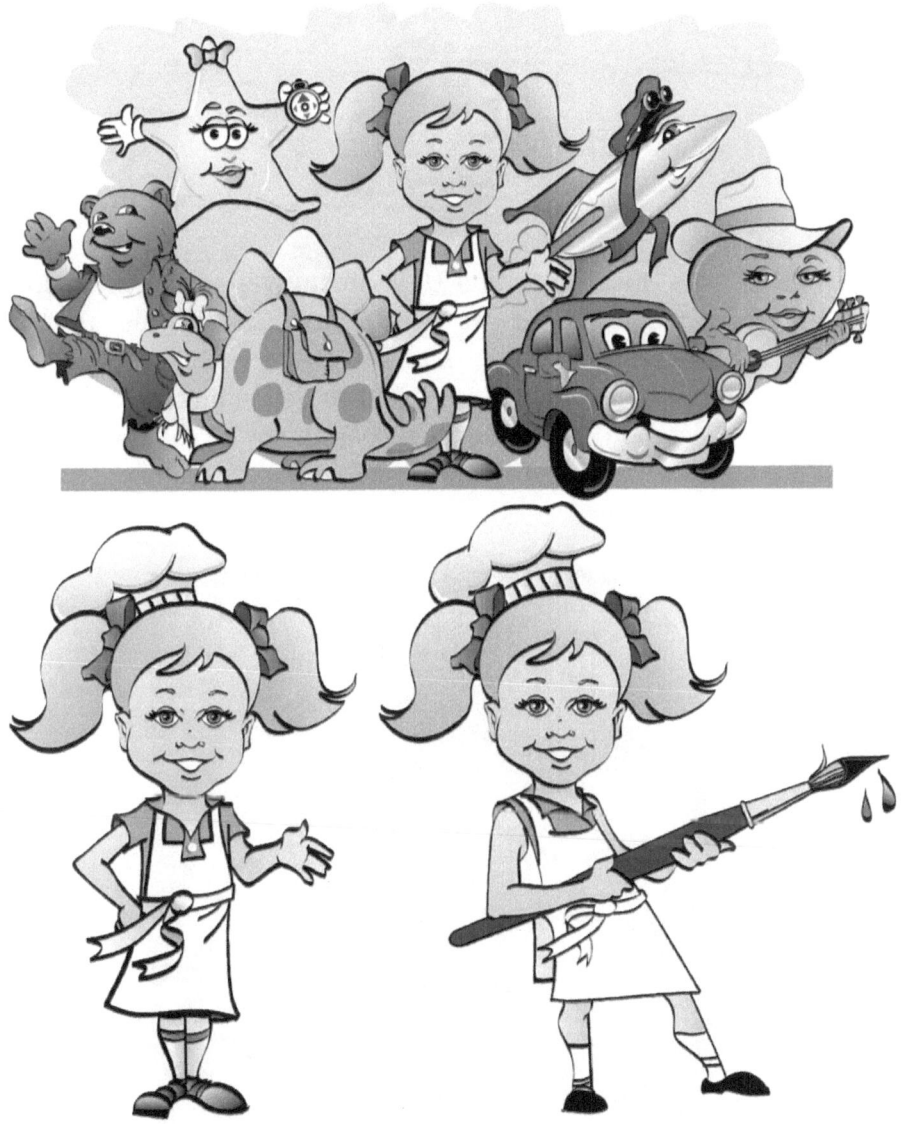

Above: a cuter style rendered in Adobe Illustrator from original
hand drawn sketches..

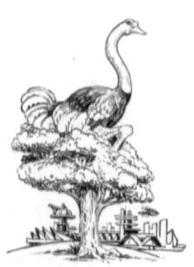

The New York State Education Department was a frequent client. Political correctness was an issue even back in the 1990's. Any group illustration required the correct racial, gender and disabilty mix. Once I had to delete any guns from a cartoon illustation for Veteran's Day after I submitted the preliminary sketch!

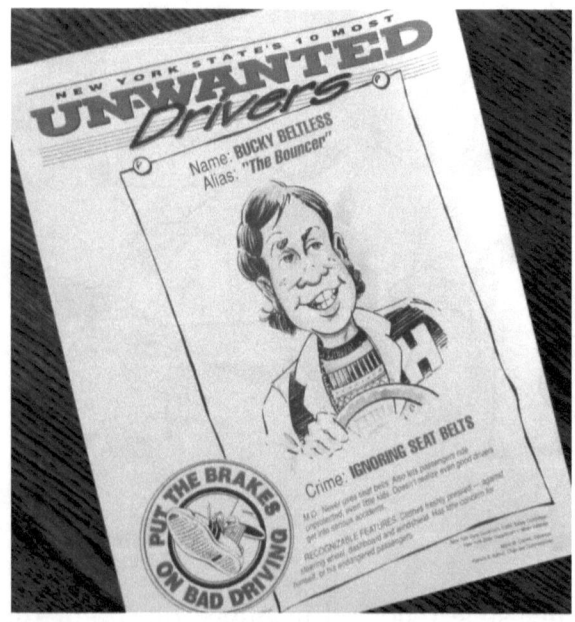

This is one of a series for New York States 10 Most Un-Wanted Drivers.

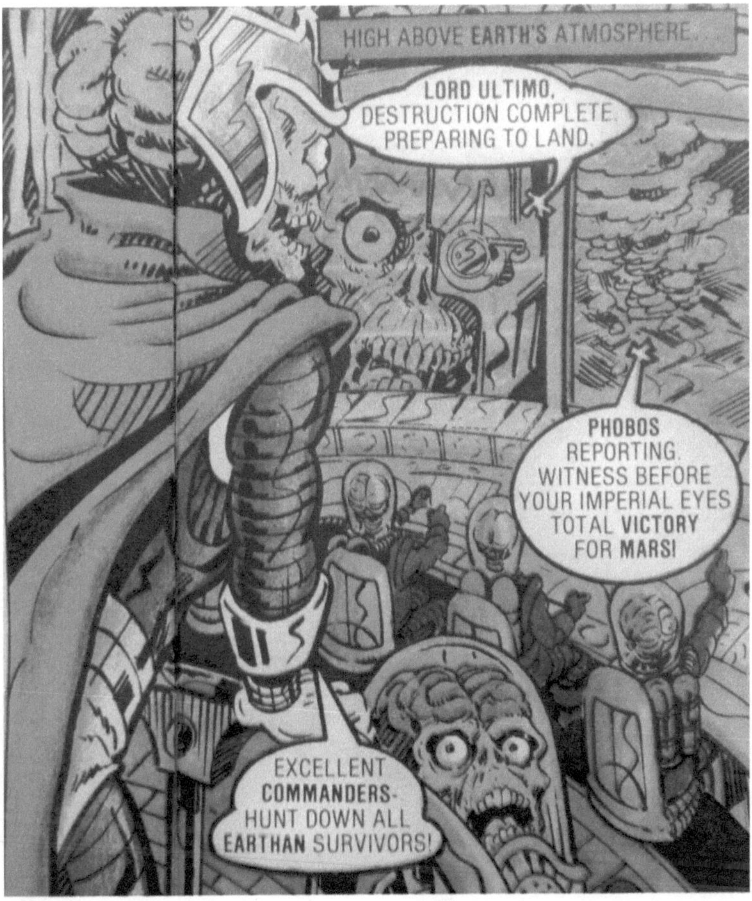

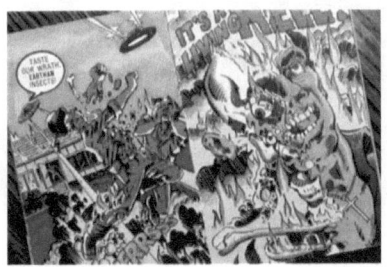

As a kid, I loved comics. This is the only time I got to do one. Shades of Jack Kirby for "Mars Attacks" pocket commix series based on the Topps cards from the 1950's. *Gruesome and hokey stuff*

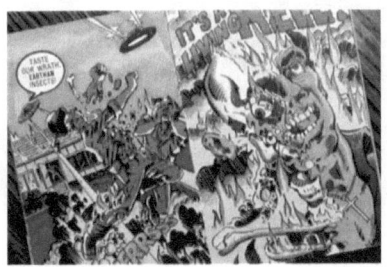

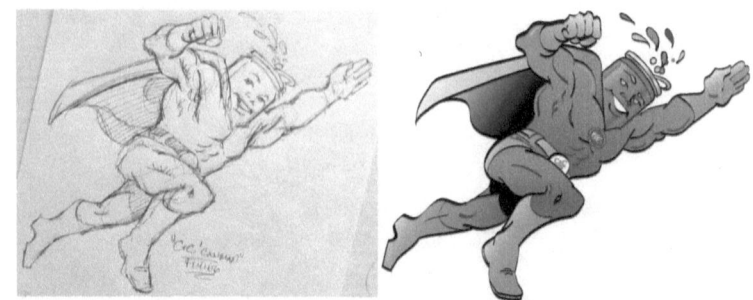

Although eventually rendered in Adobe Illustrator, all art begins on
paper in pencil or ballpoint pen.

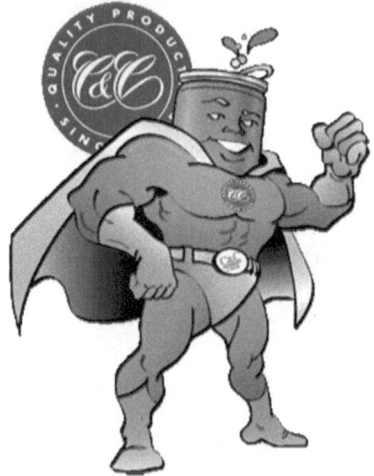

"Cola Man" for C&C Beverages. Below he is used as their FB header

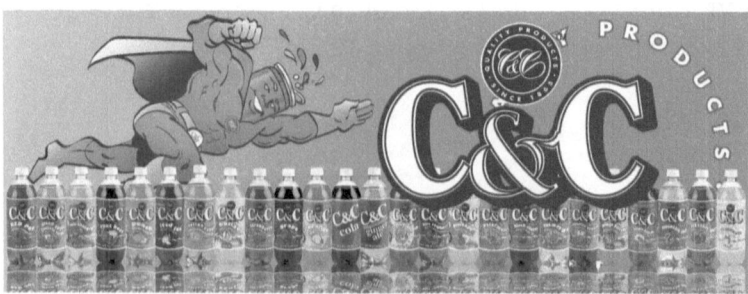

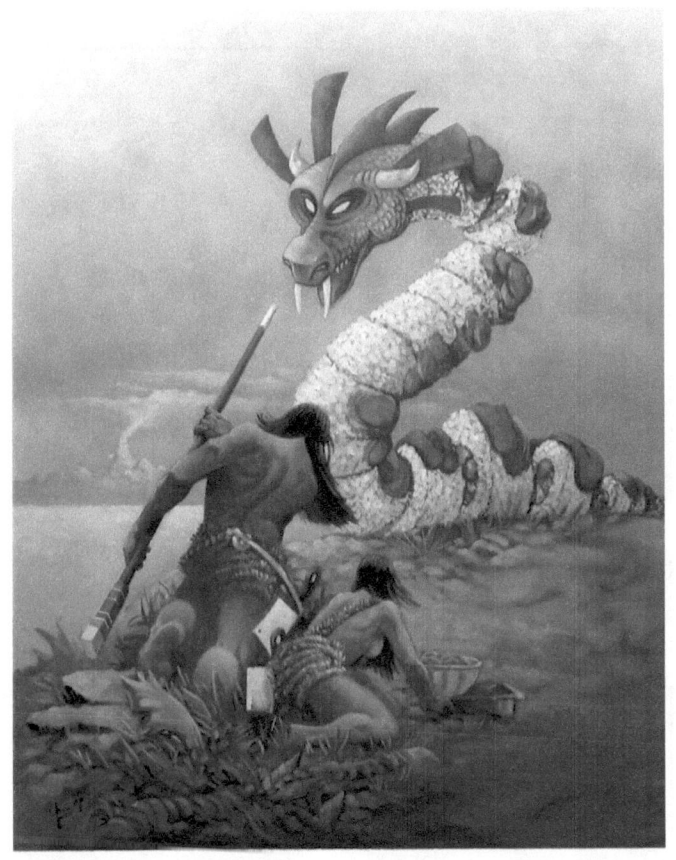

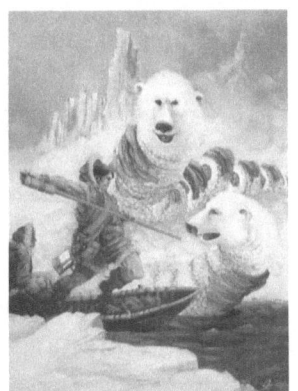

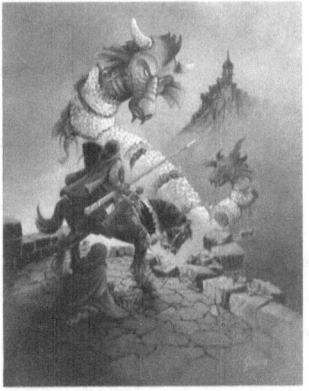

A series of illustrations for sushi – the dreaded Dragon roll!

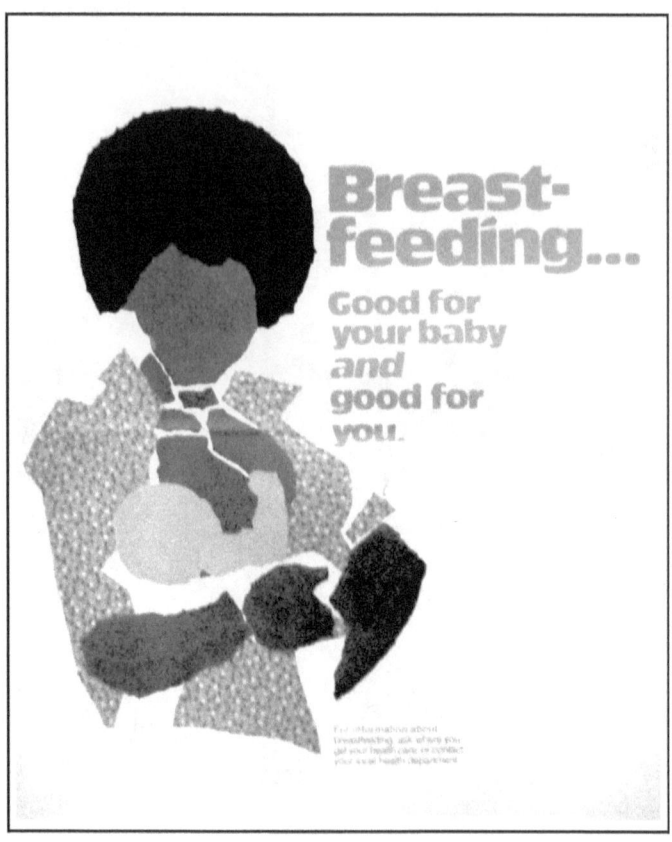

Sometimes thinking "outside the box" comes in handy. When working for D.J. Moore Advertising, in the late 1970's, we had to come up with a campaign promoting breastfeeding for the NYS Health Department. Since it was (and is now) a delicate subject, photography or realistic illustration was out of the question.

This illustration used torn paper and cut fabric as a media I had never done this style before but it worked and the client was delighted. I added the technique to my repertoire and used it several tymes for subsquent projects over the years.

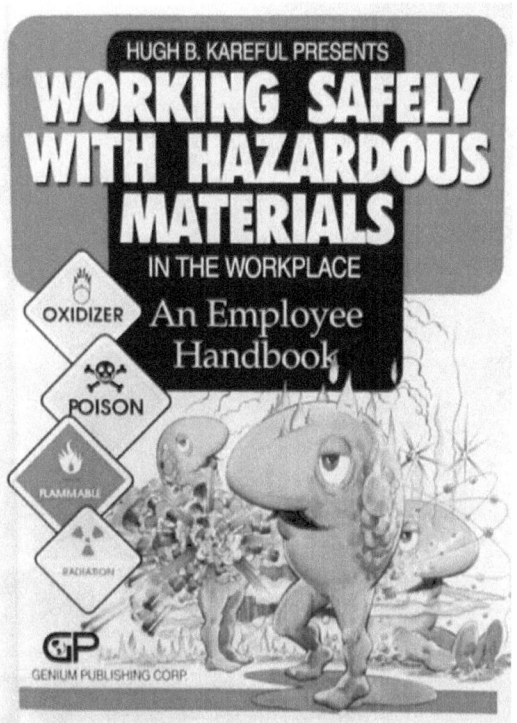

Genium Publishing Company was probably my most prolific client. I developed the character Hugh B. Kareful, who represented a hazardous material or chemical. He appreared in countless publications over the years.. The company specialized in industrial safety information. When printed material was largely replaced by digital media much of their print materials disappeared.

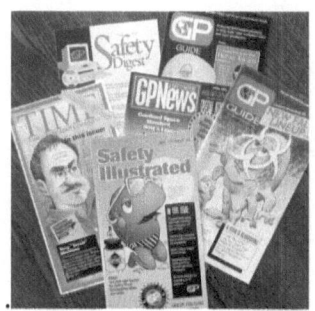

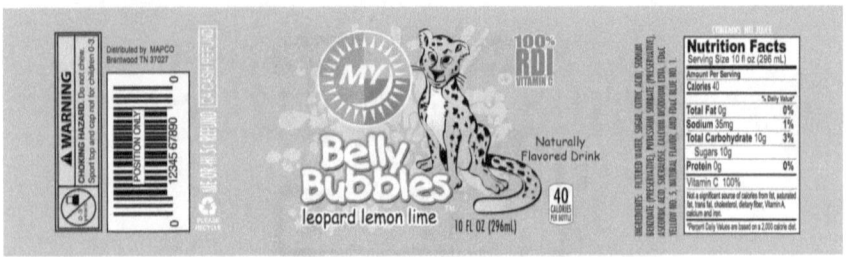

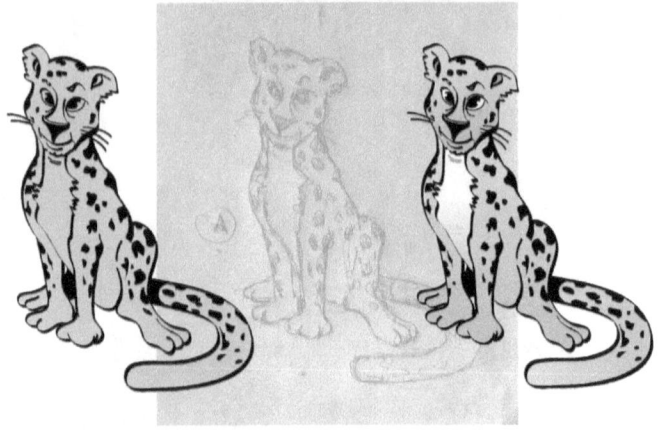

The ability to DRAW cannot be overstated. Electronic tools can enhance, simplify and save time, but the core of illustration is drawing.

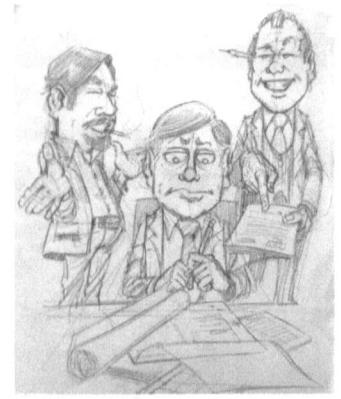

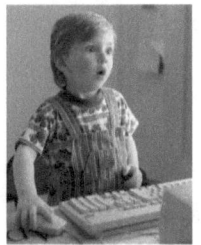

Website design:

The purpose of a website *is not to bedazzle and entertain the viewer*. Our job is to get attention, inform and communicate.

Websites should designed to be more like on-line brochures or ads, with custom graphics and attention to copy and design arrangements that function as a website, but are *quick and easy to load and navigate.*

To be effective, a website must be up to date and revised frequently to highlight new products and services. News and special events and even sales presentations placed on the site can be called-up on a laptop for sales meetings. By using contemporary techniques such as slide shows, more information and products can be presented without a lot of "clicking around"

Care must be taken NOT to use very new technology that few people have and may be asked to download. Most of the time the average person won't do this because it is time consuming or they fear a computer problem. Often they will just click off to another site. ALWAYS design to the lowest common denominator.

NOTE: In some cases, techniques like flash or slide shows will not translate well to portable devices such as phones or tablets.

NOTE: ALL photos should be "optimized for web" for fast load times using Photoshop – in 72 DPI (Dots Per Inch.)

A small client of mine in Phoenix said to me: "I have some inquiries from prospective new distributors about our product lines from the trade show we just went to. What can we send them quickly?"

I responded by saying: "That is why we built a website for you... send them the link"

Websites rarely exist to be "found" by search engines but they are a valuable and fast way to present who you are and what you do. Like an on-line brochure without the printing or mailing expense. And unlike brochures, they can be updated instantly at minimal cost. In all communications – "All roads lead to the website."

They should easy to navigate, fast to load, and easy to understand.

It is VERY important to note that search engines look for text, not graphics. Often people searching for a company or product that I have done design work for wind up landing at my website and sending inquiries to me via e-mail because I have a lot of text in the website!

I once did a website for a small children's bookstore. It's Google page rank was low until I added one small link to a page that contained their business plan (minus any personal or proprietary information) and they shot up to page one or two on a Google search of pertinent key words: bookstore, children, Phoenix, toys, books.

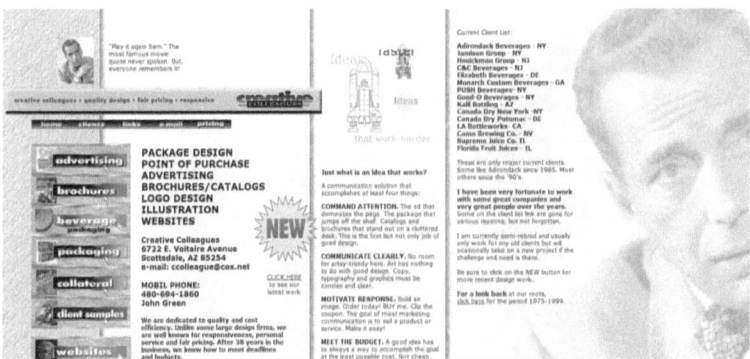

www.creativecolleagues.com. Note the large navigation "roll-over" flash buttons and the animation in the center. Although it's designed to fit wide screens, its column format can easily be viewed on small formats like tablets or phones.

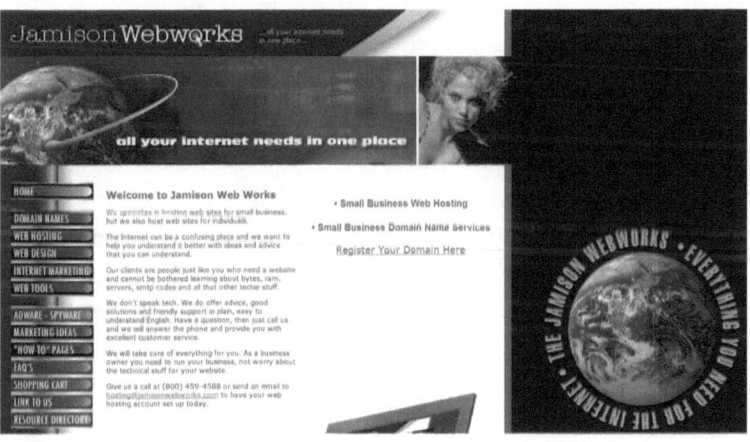

This site for Jamison Webworks in NY has many link buttons to the multitude of services they offer. The links are on EVERY page and in the same position so viewer can easily return or move on to other pages of interest. www.jamisonwebworks.com

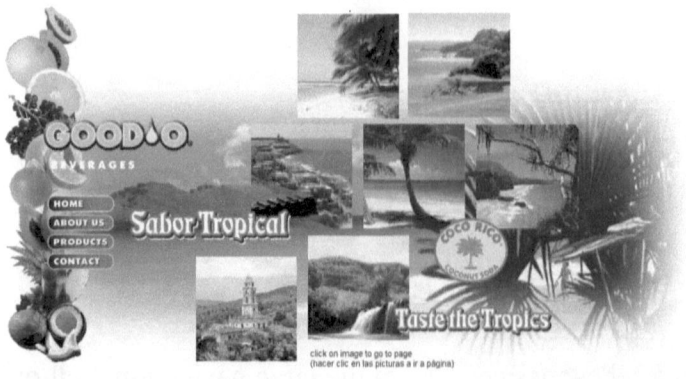

This is one of the larger sites I have done. The home page above has only four navigation buttons, that are common to all pages, but since the site is Spanish and English, most pages also have navigation links to Spanish language sections.

The seven tropical island photos "roll over" (a technique commonly used for navigation buttons only) when a cursor passes over them revealing photos of a major product groups they offer. Each product page also has photos of tropical island scenes that "roll over" in the same fashion. Clicking in the "products" link navigation button brings the viewer to a similar page but with all the product photos revealed! They in turn link to pages with information regarding each product offering.

NOTE: Originally designed in 2004, it was updated often, as their product lines changed. The site has since been discontinued.

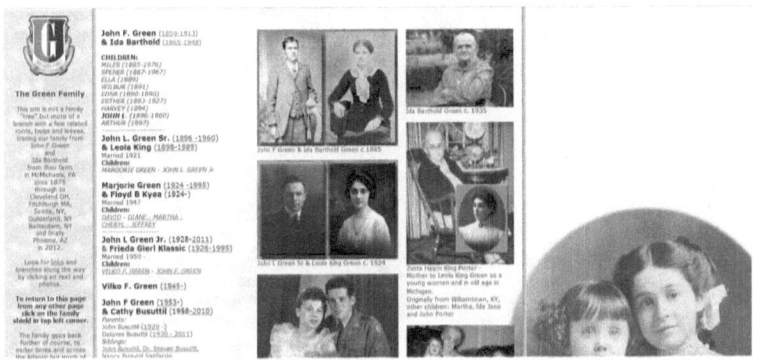

A large family tree website with many links and all the features of previously shown sites.

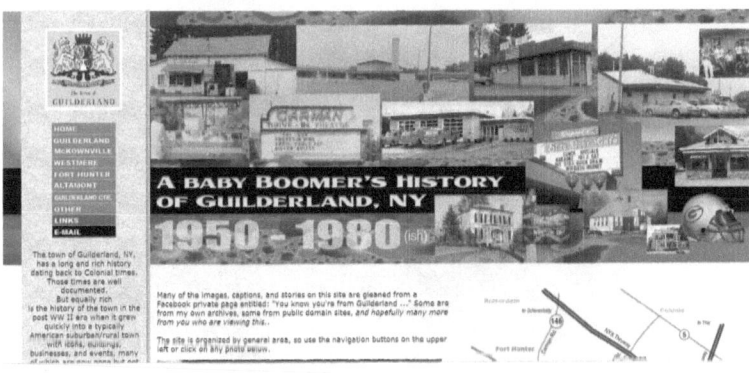

A site designed for people from the town of Guilderland, NY

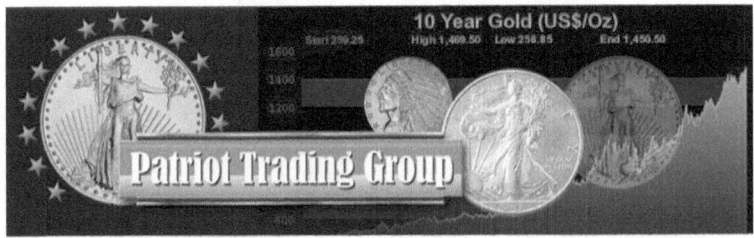

I designed only the header for this site www.allamericangold.com

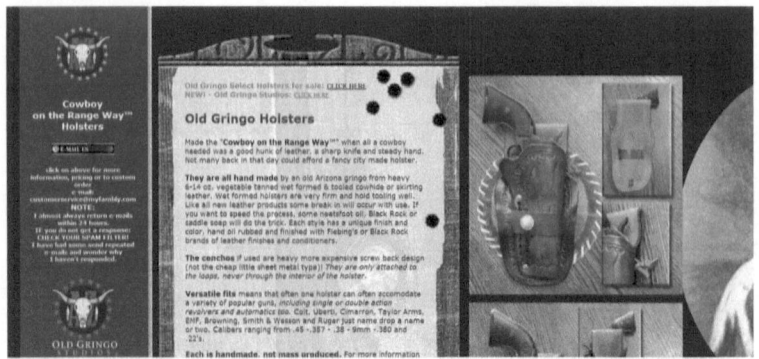

Old Gringo Holsters, a sales site for hand made leather gun holsters. www.oldgringoholsters.com – Again, note the column format.

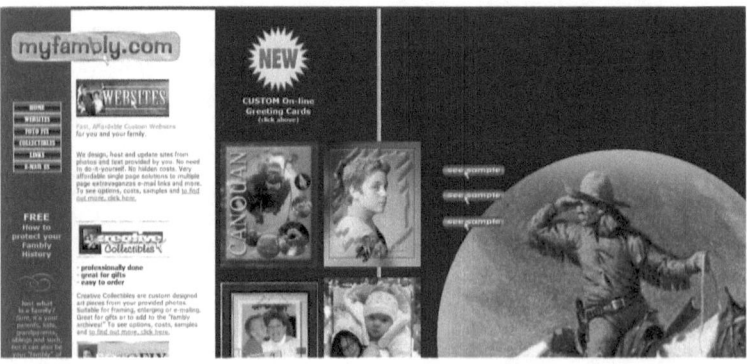

This site sells a multitude of services to families and individuals: www.myfambly.com

All of the sites follow the same general principles noted above but each has its own unique look and purpose. Note that ALL are designed to accommodate small vertical devices as well as wide screen monitors.

Below are links to some of the other sites I have done:
www.nyravioli.com - www.canouandivecenter.com
www.ashforkaz.com - www.jgreenbooks.com.com

Logo Design

A company logo, once known as their trademark, is usually the first and last impression left on the customer. And like any other good piece of design, it needs to meet certain criteria:

IMPACT: An effective logo design must be distinctive *and legible* at any size, from a postage stamp to the side of a tractor-trailer. And while color is important, a good design must be just as clear in black & white or in only one color.

COMMUNICATION: Much like good journalism, a logo must clearly state: *who, what* and *why*!

The WHO may seem to be obvious. The name the company or organization. But unless the company is GE, IBM or AT&T avoid the reliance on acronyms if at all possible unless it has real significance or is very well established. MADD (Mothers Against Drunk Drivers) is one good example. If an acronym *must* be used, be sure to include the full name of the organization in a clear and readable font especially during a change of design or the introductory period.

WHAT is the nature of the product or service? Whenever possible, show or demonstrate the product or service symbolically or pictorially. For example, a logo for a limousine service could show a vehicle and or people being driven to and from a destination. A symbol can also allude to the name of the company. Apple computer and Shell Oil are good examples. In any case, the symbol should not be so abstract or obscure that it requires explanation or become a brainteaser. Often a symbol or pictorial element *is not needed*. The name of the company, product or organization in a distinct typeface, perhaps slightly modified may be the best solution.

WHY is the nature of not only the company, but also the nature of their audience *and* their customers. What is the nature of the organization or individual in terms of adjectives: Conservative? Contemporary? Glamorous? Old Fashioned? Humorous? Elegant? Strong? Flamboyant? - the list goes on.

When possible the design should be timeless. Many logos have evolved or changed over the years. Pepsi is a good example from the script typeface of its early years to the "ying and yang" circular element and all the variants they use today. And even today, the company plays with and offers variants at every turn. Some like Coca Cola (or Coke), have changed very little. Some like GE (General Electric) have remained the same.

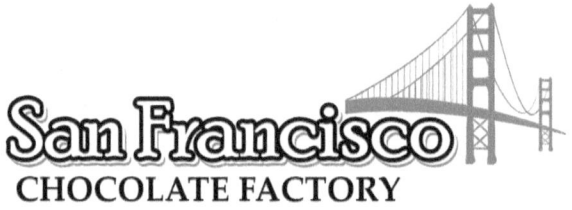

Chocolate is hard to make into a symbol – San Francisco – no problem. The Golden Gate bridge is a common icon.

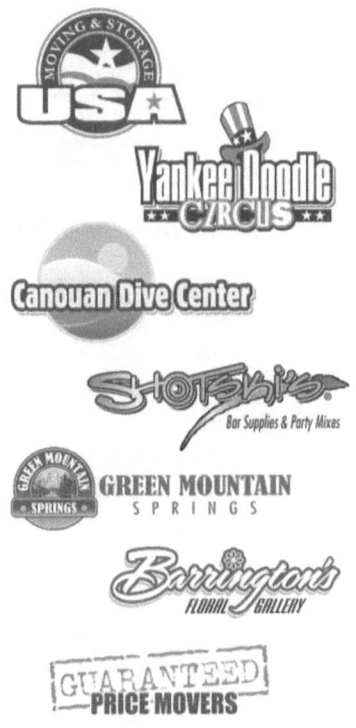

Above are some of the various logo designs I have done over the years. While they hold up in black and white, color is inherent to the impact of all of them. See them in color at:

www.creativecolleagues.com/logos.htm

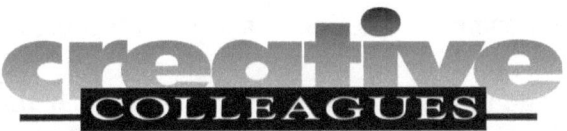

Following my own advice, this logo was designed in 1992 when the company was formed and is still in use today. There has never been any need to change it, despite the occasional irrational urge to do so.

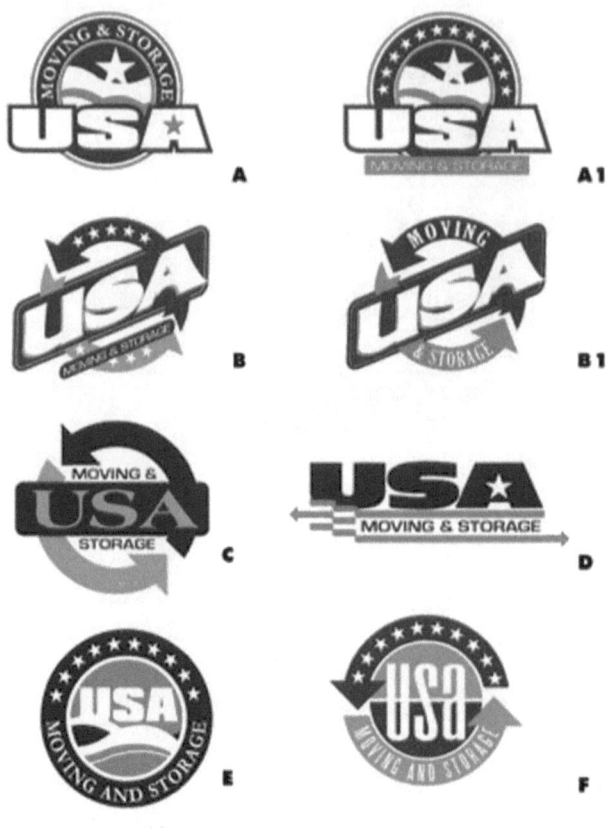

Knowing your client is sometimes an unfair advantage.

Although I submitted several options (versions B through F), I knew that being ardent Barak Obama supporters in 2004, they would choose A or A1 which resembled his campaign logo. From a personal standpoint, it did not matter to me because they were all reasonable solutions. The variants were useful however as comparisons and contrasting ideas.

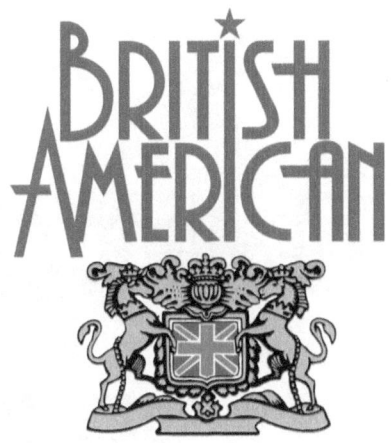

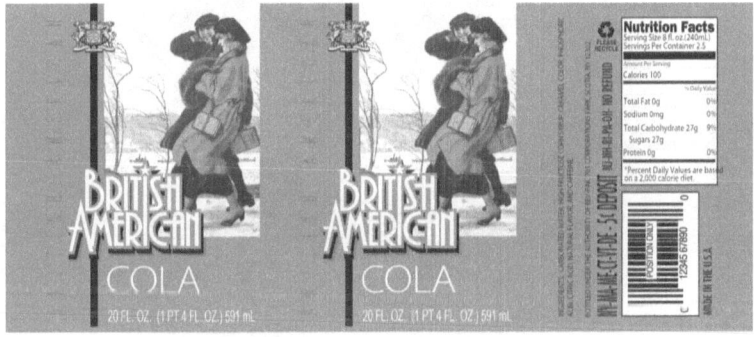

Sometimes you have to combine an existing logo element with other treatments to update a product.

In this case, the coat of arms seal had existed but had become rather dated in its use and did not carry the brand image sufficiently by itself. Used here in conjunction with a type treatment to match the 1920's look of the illustrations and package design. You will see this as it applied to the entire flavor line in the package design a previous chapter.

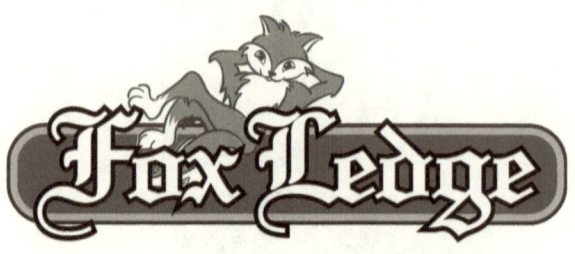

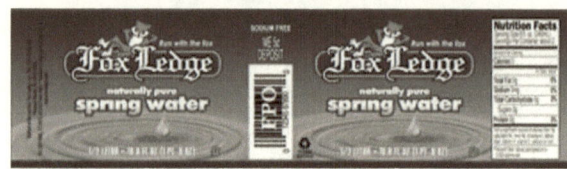

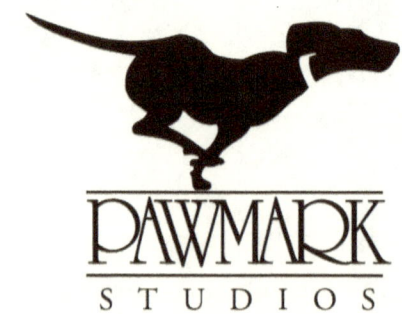

These both use animal imagery to carry the concept:

Fox Ledge Springs in Fox Ledge, Pennsylvania
Pawmark Studios, my original company – *"Pawmark, when you only care enough to send the very least."*

Career Options
Employed or self-employed, that is the question.

There are advantages to both of these options depending on your personality and financial situation.

Get a job!

If you want or need the security of a steady paycheck or you are just beginning in the business this may be your best option. Just remember the *opportunities concept* I mentioned at the beginning of this book. Follow the opportunities that lead to forward motion in your career even if they are not exactly where you eventually want to be. No matter where you are in your career, if you want the security of a job, are not disciplined enough to manage your time on your own or just feel more comfortable being an employee that is perfectly fine!

The downside of this is that you will also get all of the drawbacks: fixed hours, conflicts with fellow employees or supervisors, needing to be part of "the team," commuting, and sometimes contractual restrictions.

And the *ultimate drawback*: If you are fired or laid off, you lose your entire source of income. Agencies and studios are often forced to let personnel go if they lose a major account or two. Working "in-house" in a corporate communications or advertising department can be just as volatile if they decide to outsource to freelancers, an agency or studio. Employees for them are a big financial liability. In those situations you will often also have non-creative types constantly looking over your shoulder with "helpful suggestions" that are hard to ignore within the company hierarchy.

All of that being said, if you are just beginning or about to begin *I recommend getting a job*. Learn everything there is to be learned in that position and then you can move on if you wish or have an opportunity to do so.

Going freelance or starting your own business

"Gee, you are so lucky to be self employed and be your own boss!" If I had a dollar for every time I heard that, I could have retired sooner. I try to explain to those folks that it is a double-edged sword and cuts both ways. For the sake of clarity and brevity, I will list the advantages and disadvantages as bulleted items below:

Freelance self-employed upsides:

• An opportunity to make more money
• If you lose a client or two, you have lost only a portion of your income – not all of it.
• You can fire a client – if you can afford to.
• No daily commute because you usually work at home.
• A flexible work schedule.

Freelance self-employed downsides:

• Your income will go up and down like a yo-yo. You have to save when the money rolls in for the times when it doesn't. And those times are impossible to predict.
• You have as many bosses as you have clients
• You get to pay almost double in social security and Medicare taxes – yours and the employer portion.
• No paid vacation. You pay for your vacation while also not making any money while you are away.
• No paid sick time. If you are sick, you work or you make no money.
• You usually have to hire an accountant to file your taxes.
• Working nights and weekends will happen – a lot!
• You need the discipline to work on work time and do household

chores on non-work time. If your spouse, significant live-in other or roommate calls you at 2:00 in the afternoon and asks you to mow the lawn or throw in a load of laundry because you are home, you must be able to say: "I am at work now. I will do it after 5:00." (or later if you are swamped and on a deadline.)

In addition to the above, if you have your own business with employees:
• Payroll and payroll taxes
• When things are slow – they must get paid *but you might not*. Laying off good people is hard and they may be hard to replace when business gets better.
• Rent or mortgage on an office.
• Repairs and maintenance
• Supplies and equipment for each person.
• If they screw up YOU are responsible.
• Spending more time as a manager, human resource director or salesman than as a creative person.

I am sure I missed a few things, but you get the general idea. Having read this you may wonder why I went the route that I did. Actually I did all of the above at one point in my career but happily for the past 16 years have been in the individual self employed mode, mostly sitting at one of several computers or drawing boards in what was designed to be a living room in my house in Phoenix, Arizona. My commuted thanks to the technology of today is something like twenty yards from bedroom to office.

The reasons that trumped all others? More money and more flexible time to pursue other interests.

Business Tips:

For those of you wanting to start your own business or for reference when you decide to do so below are the three most important things I learned along the way:

• **Relationships:** When I was a rookie and one day was about to play delivery boy to bring a bunch of artwork to a printer, I asked my boss, Don Moore: *"Why do we so frequently use this particular printer? Are they always the best price?"*

He responded: *"Not always but they are competitive. We use them frequently because I have a relationship with them so that when one of our clients call on a Friday afternoon and want their brochures printed and delivered by Monday, I know they will do it for me because of that relationship."*

I never forgot that pearl of wisdom he imparted to me that day. Many businesses constantly shop only price and consequently hop from company to company to save a nickel here or there *but they build no relationships or most importantly: loyalty.*

Long-term relationships are important. It is always easier to keep a client than find another BUT the most important reason is that you get to know what they need and they know that you will understand that and trust you to fulfill that need.

Whenever I had a personal crisis in my life my long-term clients (whom often eventually became personal friends) understood, and supported me until the crisis passed!

Once, not many years ago a client of mine was financially screwing another client I have had a business and personal relationship with since 1985, The Jamison Group. When he continued to do so, I resigned the account and told him why. And not in kindly words.

When a client asked me to send artwork to another printer, I called the printer who was doing the work and whom I have been working with since 1982, and asked if they had been paid. When they said no, I refused to send the electronic art to the new printer. The client was furious but I didn't care. (He had tried to stiff me too!)

Loyalty

Hand in glove with relationships is loyalty. Loyalty to your clients and your vendors yields good business and good feelings. And you sleep better at night!

Once after hours I was alone in the office packing up a box of artwork to send out when the phone rang. I picked it up and Doug Martin, the General Manager of Adirondack Beverages was on the other end. Since I rarely dealt with him directly, I wondered what the "problem" was going to be. He said: "Hey John, I just wanted to call to tell you how much we appreciate you and your staff busting hump to get this project out for us. It is an important piece of business to us. So thanks again." His company was paying us for the work so the call was hardly necessary, BUT his gentlemanly attitude and words of thanks further cemented an already valuable relationship.

Often over the years when swamped with projects and trying to decide which to work on next, these relationships often come into play. Long after Adirondack Beverages ceased to be my largest client financially, when they asked me to jump, my response always was and always is: "How high?"

I work for many clients that are competitors. Great care is taken to keep their plans and secrets: SECRET. Otherwise, I would be history in a hurry.

Integrity

This often means doing the right thing even if it does not make financial sense, or just because it's the right thing to do. Keeping commitments, following through, and most importantly: being honest.

Once when I was also being the printing broker for many of my clients and earning 15% on every print job, I was approached by one of the printers and asked if I would be willing to raise the quoted price in return for a "kick-back" commission. I refused because I felt it was unethical, although it was very tempting financially. Not long after that, I found out that the general manager of one of my clients was just fired in part because he was doing this. With the same, guy who had approached me!

NOTE: Although lucrative, I soon got out of the print brokering business, because if the client fails to pay you, YOU are still on the hook to the printer. On a $50,000 print run, you not only lose your $7,500 commission you now OWE 50 grand to the printer!

I have also made a lot of money over the years by NOT making money. Sometimes a client will ask me to do a project and upon reflection, I will tell them that the project or the way they planned to do it was unnecessary or too expensive. Or there was a better, cheaper way to do it. In the short term, it cost me some money but in the long term, it gave me the most valuable thing you can get from a client: TRUST. Along with that, trust comes loyalty and relationship and those two things can make you a lot of money.

Billing and business

Nowadays, I am still occasionally asked what my hourly rate is. I respond to this inquiry thus: "Ten thousand, four hundred, sixty seven dollars and 18 cents per hour." After the silence on the other end of the phone settles in for a moment, I tell them: "BUT, I will do your project in about 17 minutes." I then go on to explain that hourly rate is relatively meaningless. If someone only charges $20 per hour, they are no bargain if they take fifty hours to complete the job. And chances are if they are that inexpensive, they are also probably not very good.

Now to be candid, when I started out I also billed by the hour and I set that rate well below the going agency rate. At a time when agency creative rates were $65-$85 per hour, I set mine at $40. As time went on the rates for both changed and are now much higher, but with time and experience, I found benchmarks and now charge by the project instead of by the hour. Consequently, my "hourly" income fluctuates between $50 an d$550 per hour.

Below is the rate structure and parameters I have posted on my website and unchanged for about 10-12 years.

"So what will this cost?" is a typical question asked by new and old clients alike. All design projects are custom solutions. There are too many variables in any project to allow for an off-the-shelf price tag. It is bit like asking: "How much does a typical house cost?"
Over the years however, I have been able to develop certain guidelines and ranges based on the overall parameters of the project. The guide below will give you some of the most common cost issues and typical design and production costs.

These are presented only as a guide. Most projects are estimated and budgeted before they begin. If alterations of the overall parameters of the project arise during production, clients are alerted to approve or re-think any additional costs likely to be incurred.

The number one cause of cost over-runs is what I call the "up a little lower" syndrome... requests for endless, minute, and often arbitrary alterations and variations. This is followed closely by changing production requirements in mid-stream. For example: A design for a full color label on metallic paper must be altered significantly to accommodate a 3-color screen-printed ACL bottle.

PRICING:

GENERAL PARAMETERS:

Cost considerations:

1. Size and scope of project
2. How many design variants and number of alterations.
3. Custom photography or stock
4. Custom illustration or stock
5. Research/travel/meetings

PACKAGE PROJECTS:

Most packaging/label designs are two-level cost issues. There is a fee for the original design concept, and upon approval of this, a separate cost for each item in the overall line.

Typical food/beverage project for a LARGE FULL LINE of products including multiple packaging venues:

BASE DESIGN DEVELOPMENT INCLUDING 3-5 DESIGN DIRECTIONS, REFINEMENTS AND FINAL PROOFS (INCLUDES E-MAIL VIEW FILES, ONE OR TWO REVISIONS AND FINAL PROOFS)

$1,800 - $3,800

FINAL EXECUTION OF APPROVED DESIGN FOR EACH SKU-
ELECTRONIC ART AND PROOFS TO PRINTER(s) AND
COORDINATION WITH VENDOR(s)

$125 - $285 ea.

DOES NOT INCLUDE TAXES IF APPLICABLE, SHIPPING,
ELECTRONIC MEDIA OR OTHER ADDITIONAL
MISCELLANEOUS EXPENSE. FOR NEW CLIENTS A
REFUNDABLE RETAINER OF $500 AND A PURCHASE ORDER
IS REQUESTED UPON PROJECT INITIATION.

Typical food/beverage project for a SMALL OR SINGLE ITEM line
of products:

$400 - $900

COLLATERAL PROJECTS:

Point-of purchase:

posters - $300 - $500

shelf talkers - $285 - $625

static clings- $175 - $500

Logos:

$300 - $900

Brochures:

6 panel - $800 - $1,200

2 sided sell-sheets - $250 - $400

Multiple page - by quotation

Websites:

$800 - $3,500

Newsletters:

$50 - $175/page

Print media ads:

small - $195 - $250

large - $500 - $800

As you can see, there is a wide range of costs in any project. Some cost saving considerations include:

1. supplying copy/text on disk or e-mail
2. viewing preliminaries via e-mail
3. avoiding travel/meetings
4. avoid changing parameters and minimizing arbitrary alterations.

Summary

I hope you have found this book entertaining as well as useful. There are many "How to" books and websites about job searches, career choices and very specific and technical guides to individual segments of the industry and topics presented here. This is meant to be an overview of much of the business based on my career.

From anecdotal evidence and statistical analysis, most if not all of the other 119 students who sat the lecture in the class noted in the introduction of this book are not in this business. Many never even got through the four years in the art program. If it comes to that, most of my professional colleagues, employees and co-workers from the first half of my career are now selling, insurance, cars, real estate or pursuing other careers.

I have often speculated on: "What if I did something else with my career?" Beach bum, mountain man, politician, or world traveler and raconteur all seem like they might have been fun. But as Don Corleone said in "The Godfather," – " that was my life and I don't apologize for it..." Or better yet, to quote an old friend and professional illustrator I once knew: "It's not a bad way to make a living."

PLEASE NOTE: All of the examples in this book are reproduced in black and white because of the budget constrictions of "print on demand" paperback books. *Some are quite old and the reproduction quality may be a bit off.*

If you want to see color, renditions and much more please visit: www.creativecolleagues.com. Feel free to use the e-mail link buttons judiciously if you have questions. Because I am semi retired and spend half my time nowadays at my 40 acre ranch in northern Arizona with no running water, electric lines or internet connection it may take me a while to get back to you.

Addendum:

As one further note on creativity: Sometimes despite the advice given here, you just have to "wing it." In 1988 after spending the previous day and night in a hospital attending the birth of my first son, I arrived bleary eyed at a photo studio for a scheduled session to do a shoot for a vending machine front. I had no layout, no idea and no clue. What I had was a lot of cans of product and studio time. The photographer and I played around for a bit with some acrylic panels and the product until we hit upon a solution. A layer of cans with one missing was placed on one sheet and it was spritzed with water and glycerin. A second layer was added with one can tilted near the empty space. The bottom layer was bottom lit so the single can seemed to be popping right off the front. It was one of the best and most unique vending fronts I ever did.

Acknowledgements:

I would be remiss if I did not thank all of my clients past and present for the experiences and insights portrayed in this book. Of special thanks: Paul Krauss, my high school art teacher, friend, second father and mentor, Jack Slutsky, and Jim O'Brien with whom I collaborated with for many clients and some of the projects seen here.

And of course, as mentioned in the dedication, the late Donald J. Moore Sr. my first and best employer from whom I learned many of the things presented here.

If I have missed anyone, I apologize and am willing to forget about it if you are!

Appendix:

THE SOFT DRINK INDUSTRY EXPOSED:

I have worked closely with many major bottlers in the soft drink industry for over 40 years. Rubbed elbows with owners, sales people, biochemists, marketing and production people. This is my inside view:

THE INDUSTRY: The business has been around a long time and as businesses go, it exists in a fairly small world. Most of the major and minor players have been in the biz for a long time and know many of their competitors and major players. Mostly in a friendly way. Like many other industries, it has undergone big changes in the past 30 years, including consolidations and technological revolutions. One of my clients has a can line that running at top speed can pack a case (24 cans) a SECOND. Inventories, shipping and production are tracked electronically on hand held devices.

Most of the mid-level regional bottlers I have worked with are very involved with community charities from food banks to universities. And they employ a LOT of people, including product and marketing managers, development staff, transportation, floor production and a host of support people.

The industry also supports a LOT of suppliers. Bottle makers, cardboard, label and can printers, trucking companies just to name a few. And yes, advertising and graphic design people.

PRODUCTS: When I started, soda including regular and diet was about 80-85% of the market. Colas, orange, root beer, ginger ale and the like. Since then that market share has flattened and diminished to be replaced by a plethora of products to meet consumer demands.

Vitamin enhanced drinks, electrolyte enhanced sports drinks, purified water, spring water, seltzers, flavored calorie free waters, energy drinks, iced teas, lemonades... this list is almost endless and continues to grow.

Consumers have more choices today than any industry owner or manager could imagine in 1981.

THE WATER: Of course, the main ingredient of any soft drink is water. It is not tap water! If you could see the purification process, the water goes through before becoming orange soda you would want a system yourself. Of course, you would shell out tens of thousands of dollars.

Spring water and purified water are available in sizes from 1/2 liter to 5-gallon dispensers. There are strict rules regarding source and nomenclature regarding these products. Beware: just because it comes in a bottle don't assume it is spring water unless it is called that ON the label. Many people think Dasani and Aquafina brands are spring waters. They are purified water from municipal sources.

If anyone had walked into my or one of my client's offices 20 years ago and suggested putting water in a bottle and selling it we would have laughed them all the way to the door.

CALORIES: Yes. Regular soft drinks have a lot of calories. Two things to consider: 1. Soft drinks were originally viewed as a treat to be had once in a while. Not gulped and guzzled like they are today. 2. When the FDA/NLEA laws were enacted in 1992-93 the soft drink industry hopped right on board quickly to update their labels. I know this because I was doing the art for them. By now, everyone is well familiar with the Nutrition Facts Panel, which is on almost every food and beverage package today. Later on, when the first lady got on a crusade for the clear on calories program many bottlers took this up also even though it was not mandatory!

And this despite the fact that the panel that developed the label guidelines apparently ignored the standard serving sizes established by the FDA, which cause a lot of recalculations and new labels.

The industry has been singled out as though it is the only contributor of overweight persons despite all of the other food products that contribute just as much or more to obesity and the associated health problems, we are seeing today.

Sugar used to be the standard sweetener. It has been largely replaced by high fructose corn syrup and/or sugar as prices fluctuate. Many high-end soft drinks now use once vilified but now redeemed sugar and sometime supplement this with honey. The jury is still out on HFCS.

CAFFEINE: Most soft drinks do NOT have caffeine. This misconception was started by an advertising campaign by Seven Up many years ago that said "No caffeine - never had it - never will." This translated into the average person thinking that ALL soft drinks had caffeine.

Only a few categories have caffeine and all are required to declare it on the package. Colas, Dr. Pepper type drinks, Mountain Dew type and all of the spin offs have caffeine. As do energy drinks. There are also some surprising exceptions. Sunkist Orange soda has a lot of caffeine. Almost no other orange soda has caffeine! I have also run across a few other exceptions in my career but they are very few.

Most cola marketers made great haste to offer caffeine free versions, when consumers wanted a cola taste, but without the caffeine jitters.

ARTIFICIAL SWEETENERS: The demand for diet drinks brought about saccharin at first. When this fell out of favor, aspartame came into play. It however had a very short shelf life and was found to be detrimental to Phenylketonurics. (try pronouncing that one). Products that have this were and are required to post a warning on the label. More recently, combinations of sucralose and acesulfame potassium (ace K) are being used. They generally have less after taste, a much longer shelf life and contain no phenylalanine.

More recently, we have seen a dramatic rise in the use of Stevia, and Stevia blends, a natural organic sweetener from South America. I personally worked on one of the early brands, which used Stevia, which was unfortunately a product ahead of its time.

PRICING: Very few consumer categories have held the price line better than soft drinks. Compare what you spent 20 years ago for a bottle of soda to today and you will see a very small increase. In fact, because of competition from regional and private label (store) brands, prices for National brands have even dropped! Now compare this to the increase in other consumer products like coffee, cereal, milk, cars or gasoline. Only consumer electronics have better.

PACKAGING: To help contain costs, the industry is constantly finding ways to use less and less plastic, aluminum and paper. Smaller labels, caps, lids and trays. A good friend of mine recently complained about how THIN the plastic was getting in water bottles. Thin is good. Aluminum cans are now as thin as they can possibly be (I think) and still hold the product in.

What about the "good old days" of glass?

Well, for starters, while glass is a very nice and easily recycled material, carbonated beverages in glass bottles were

DANGEROUS. Especially in larger sizes! When dropped the carbonation held inside released quickly and turned bottles into fragmentation grenades. Glass is also very heavy and consumes much more fuel to transport.

Cans when I started were made of 3 piece steel. Printed flat, the can was then formed and sealed at one edge. Then the bottom was applied. After filling, the heavy top closed the product in. It was heavy and wasteful. These were replaced in the 80's with two piece-extruded aluminum. Paper thin and light but able to keep carbonation in for years, also very easy and desirable to recycle.

Plastic was just starting to come in vogue when I was starting. EVIL PLASTIC. But just go to any store today and try to find any products NOT packed in a plastic jar, bottle or tube. And mostly heavy colored plastic, which is more wasteful, and oil consuming than the ever thinner, clear soft drink bottles. Let's not even get started on the over plastic contained products that are designed that way to hang better on a hook or prevent pilfering.

I am not saying that we do not use too much plastic today, but the soft drink industry is doing its best until a better solution appears. For MYSELF, I am a fan of aluminum. Chills real fast, light and more easily recycled. And unlike plastic, it holds carbonation and freshness far better than plastic.

STUPIDITY: Now I HAVE run into some stupidity in my career including dumb products or packaging or both.

Some of my favorites:

- Caffeinated water. This originated as a product for stockbrokers who were only allowed water on the stock exchange floor. Problem is that caffeine is an organic substance and unless packed under extremely sterile circumstance it could start to grow things.

- One fool who apparently had money to burn tried to market NUTZ Sparkling, a nut flavored soda - peanut, hazelnut, banana nut and pistachio. Thankfully it did not last. Although as a side bar Jones soda does a turkey gravy flavor around Thanksgiving.

- The product development chief at one of my clients and I were dumbfounded one day when a customer seriously asked if we could put Viagra in spring water. Despite the logical and legal arguments, he was still not convinced.

- Beverage people are generally pretty conservative folks. One time however, an owner wanted me to design a Dr Pepper knock off. There are hundreds of these on the market so the product itself was not a problem. I made the mistake however in the design process of showing him several options and included one that showed him what should NOT be done because it was too close to Dr Pepper's trade dress (i.e graphics). He insisted on using that design. I insisted on a legal waiver disclaiming ME of liability that he supplied. The product was produced and he was sued. His lawyer made a LOT of money.

- And lastly, speaking of lawyers, they single handedly killed a viable product. Back when wine coolers were soaring in popularity a client of mine decided to make a soft drink that tasted like a cooler but contained NO alcohol. Even though I had clearly and large on the FRONT of the label: "contains no alcohol" and "Contains no wine" the lawyers insisted we call the product a soda cooler. It died a quick death.

=========================

This is not meant to be an in depth study of the industry but rather a brief overview based on my 40 plus years of experience. I have been lucky in my career to learn about a lot of different industries:

food, electronics, industrial products, hotels, government and commercial real estate just to name a few BUT soft drinks have been the core of my career. For the most part I have found the industry itself and the people involved with it imperfect to be sure but by in large responsible, hardworking, interesting and rewarding to work with.

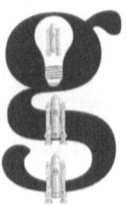

ABOUT THE AUTHOR

John Green is originally from Guilderland, NY, but moved to Arizona in 1999 and is a retired graphic designer, Advertising art Director, copywriter and illustrator. He spends half his time now at his 40 acre off the grid ranch in northern Arizona, occasionally joined by his lovely and forbearing wife Wendy. Many of his stories are written there during the quiet starry nights amid the howls of coyotes, hooting owls and things that go bump in the night.

For more information, and other books by this author including his best selling novella, *"Tommy Polito's Tavern,"* please go to:

www.jgreenbooks.com

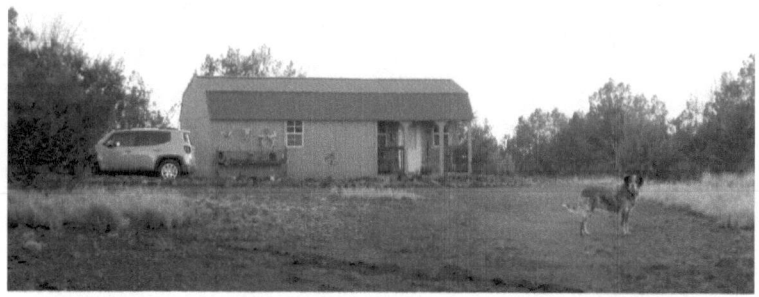

OTHER BOOKS BY J. FRANKLIN GREEN

Young Readers:
• THE WIND IN THE JUNIPERS
• LOLA, SAM AND THE JACKALOPE

Apocalyptic Fiction:
• 2035 THE ELEPHANT IN THE ROOM

Science Fiction:
• ALIEN HEREDITY
• AND THE MEEK SHALL INHERIT

Historic Fiction:
• IMMORTAL SERGEANT BACHMAN

Recovery:
• BOOZE & BETRAYAL

Non-Fiction:
•EVERYTHING I NEEDED TO KNOW ABOUT LIFE,
I LEARNED ON A BASEBALL FIELD (*Well, Almost*)
• A BABY BOOMERS HISTORY OF GUILDERLAND, NY

Supernatural mystery:
• ROADSIDE 66
• TOMMY POLITO'S TAVERN

See all at - www.jgreenbooks.com

www.ingramcontent.com/pod-product-compliance
Lightning Source LLC
Chambersburg PA
CBHW032026170526
45157CB00002B/870